IMAGES
of America

BULLOCK'S
DEPARTMENT STORE

IMAGES
of America

BULLOCK'S
DEPARTMENT STORE

Devin T. Frick

ARCADIA
PUBLISHING

Published by Arcadia Publishing
Charleston, South Carolina

Printed in the United States of America

Library of Congress Control Number: 2014949518

For all general information, please contact Arcadia Publishing:
Telephone 843-853-2070
Fax 843-853-0044
E-mail sales@arcadiapublishing.com
For customer service and orders:
Toll-Free 1-888-313-2665

Visit us on the Internet at www.arcadiapublishing.com

*To all who fondly remember, shopped at, or worked
for Bullock's and Bullocks Wilshire.*

CONTENTS

ACKNOWLEDGMENTS

I was born and raised in California and have always had a great fondness for the state's history, culture, and people. Over the years, I have been extremely fortunate to produce museum exhibits, art shows, and publications on subjects related to the Golden State. This book is near and dear to me, as Bullock's was so very much a part of my life. My grandmother purchased items from Bullock's for her home in the 1930s. She was also a proofreader for the *Los Angeles Examiner* newspaper, proofing many news articles that included society happenings and events featuring Bullock's Downtown and Bullocks Wilshire. My mother shopped at most of the major stores: J.W. Robinson's, The Broadway, May Company, I. Magnin, and Bullock's. For me, Bullock's and I. Magnin set themselves apart from the rest. Bullock's Westwood, Santa Ana, La Habra, and Pasadena were beautiful stores with equally stunning merchandise. Hand-blown glass ornaments from Russia, Waterford crystal from Ireland, Royal Doulton flambe and china from England, fine sheets and bedding, and, of course, quality clothing, were always bought at Bullock's.

No project, large or small, can be done alone. I wish to thank many individuals, libraries, historical societies, universities, and other institutions. My mother, Jean Frick, is an accredited librarian and USC alumni. Interviews and assistance came from Richard Martinez, Max Pierce, Lisa Ackerman, Darlene Quinn, David Galvan, and numerous friends. Larry Frick assisted with technical support.

Los Angeles Public Library, Pasadena Public Library, Santa Ana Public Library, Palm Springs Public Library, San Francisco Public Library, Costa Mesa Historical Society, Palo Alto Public Library, Bullock's employee publications from various years, P.G. Winnett's Store Objectives, Bullock's store interviews, *California* magazine, *Architect & Engineer*, *Architectural Forum*, *Architectural Record*, *California Arts*, the *Los Angeles Times*, the *Los Angeles Examiner*, *Pasadena Star News*, *Women's Wear Daily*, and *Orange County Illustrated* all provided information and images.

All images in this book were collected over many decades from various sources. All are in the public domain, originating in the newspapers, magazines, and community publications previously listed. Credited photographs come from Mott Studio of Los Angeles, Maynard Parker, Julius Shulman, Jerome K. Muller, and others. All images, unless otherwise noted, are from the author's collection.

FOREWORD

Perhaps no other department store reflects the 20th century more than Bullock's. Created in 1907 by a successful Los Angeles merchant named Arthur Letts, it was a speculative venture, seemingly independent, yet not. If it failed, it bore the name of the employee trusted to run it.

Bullock's was a success. It was located four blocks south of Letts's The Broadway Department Store. It would be five years after Letts's 1923 death before John G. Bullock and a trusted group of investors could wrest independence and full ownership. They did, and began work on a "suburban" branch store only a few miles west of downtown that would be unique in design, merchandising, and name from the main store, which had expanded to multiple buildings. Bullocks Wilshire opened four weeks before the October 1929 stock market crash. The store was an instant hit with millionaires and movie stars for clothing and accessories, and the fifth floor tea room would become a destination for countless ladies who lunched, regardless of social status.

In the fall of 1933, John Bullock, now a civic leader, died unexpectedly. P.G. Winnett took charge, and Bullock's prosperity continued. In 1964, Bullock's Inc. was acquired by Federated Department Stores. Around 1974, the Wilshire store and three others were spun off into an apostrophe-less division called Bullocks Wilshire, and the Bay Area had a short-lived Bullock's North division.

By 1988, Bullock's, along with sister divisions Bloomingdale's and I. Magnin & Co., were considered Federated's crown jewels both by shoppers and professionals alike. About that time, Federated became the target of a hostile takeover, resulting in Bullock's being sold to R.H. Macy & Co., and the headquarters moved to Atlanta. In 1996, Bullock's and its original parent company The Broadway were re-branded as Macy's.

The motto "To Build a Business That Will Never Know Completion" remains above the doorway of Bullocks Wilshire. This book by Devin T. Frick remains true to that statement.

—Max Pierce, former Bullock's and Federated executive,

The Bullock Ideal

To build a business that will never know completion but that will advance continually to meet advancing conditions

To develop stocks and service to a notable degree

To create a personality that will be known for its strength and friendliness

To arrange and co-ordinate activities to the end of winning confidence by meriting it

To strive always to secure the satisfaction of every customer

This is the aim of Bullock's that is being impressed more and more indelibly as the days go by upon the character of the business itself

John Bullock and his team strove to serve their patrons only the best. Every promise to a customer was a sacred obligation. Regardless of cost, the satisfaction of the patron came first. Cheerfulness and sincerity exuded from every employee and every department. Bullock's strove to create an atmosphere that would place it above the ordinary level of the average store, where friendship would be expressed through "notable service." The store developed a motto that lasted as long as the company did.

INTRODUCTION

The story of California's Bullock's department stores and the Bullocks Wilshire specialty stores begins with its founder, John Gillespie Bullock, who was born in the Paris province of Ontario, Canada, on January 14, 1871. When he was only two years old, his father, Joseph, a railroad man of Scotch ancestry, passed away, leaving his mother to take care of the family. When he was 11, John had to leave school in order to help with the family's needs, his first job being a stock boy at Rheder's Grocery for $2 a week.

Over time, John's responsibilities at Rheder's increased, and he was given a delivery wagon. With great pride in this promotion, he took to the streets, soliciting orders and delivering them. Bullock zealously guarded against any errors. Years later, he revealed, "it was my ambition while driving that delivery wagon to have, some day, as big a store as Rheder's."

At the age of 20, John received a letter from an uncle who lived in California, extolling the virtues and opportunities available out West. It lit a fire within Bullock. Sensing her son's desire, John's mother consented to the trip, giving him $150 from her small savings. In January 1896, Bullock made it across two countries and one large continent. Upon his arrival in Los Angeles, the thrifty young man deposited his money in the Citizens' National Bank. However, finding work in his new city was a difficult matter.

In February of the same year, Bullock noticed a newspaper advertisement from a store at the corner of Fourth Street and Broadway, selling a large amount of bankrupt merchandise. Bullock went down to the store early the following day to secure employment, but a large crowd had arrived and filled the store. Bullock was informed by a man at the store entrance that he had all the help he needed and that they were no longer hiring. Bullock did not take "no" for an answer, and stayed near the facility as the crowds kept coming. With so many customers, the store was forced to lock its front doors and let customers out the back. Bullock weaved through the customers to find the man who had turned him away. His persistence paid off, as the man recognized him and, amid the mayhem, asked Bullock, "Do you want to go to work now?" John was paid $2 a day as a salesman in domestics. Thus began a new future for both men.

Arthur Letts, the proprietor of The Broadway Department Store, was new to the area himself. In Bullock, Letts saw an eager and ambitious man and soon had him working in various departments, including men's furnishings, and eventually, the buying department. As time passed, Letts awarded Bullock additional roles, such as superintendent, and saw in him the makings of a fine executive, one who was truthful, temperate, and direct.

Over the next few years, The Broadway Department Store grew rapidly but haphazardly. The store itself expanded into adjoining buildings, on different levels. Expansion into a new, modern addition was in the works at the corner of Fourth Street and Broadway, but still more good fortune lay in Arthur Letts's hands.

In 1906, an Eastern-based company began building a store at Seventh Street and Broadway. The company's capital ran out, however, and the structure's steel frame was halted at the seventh floor. This Tehama building was now half-built and without a tenant. The owner had few options but to submit an offer to Arthur Letts, who was interested. Letts, however, felt that taking on the operations of another store could be difficult. Letts required that the rent on the building be kept low for the first 10 years of business. The owner, Edwin T. Earl, agreed, and Letts signed a 50-year lease on the yet-to-be-finished building. With a fully operating Broadway store just a few blocks away, John G. Bullock was put in charge of the new store at Seventh and Broadway.

Arthur Letts's confidence in Bullock led to the new store being named "The Bullock," with a stipulation that it would revert back to the Broadway name if necessary. Providing $250,000 in capital for Bullock's, Letts remained in the background, feeling that the stores should be kept completely separate. Bullock and his personally-chosen fellow Canadian, Broadway errand boy P.G. Winnett, retained full responsibility for the store from its inception.

Bullock's connections with the Broadway were severed on November 1, 1906. Arthur Letts and John Bullock did not communicate with each other until March 2, 1907, when Bullock invited Letts to see the new store prior to opening. Letts looked the store over with a smart eye and upfront criticism. The surrounding streets were in gridlock as thousands visited the new store. A large rooftop marquee illuminated the night sky. A newspaper described the opening gala: "2,500 people flocked to the opening of Bullock's mammoth department store and packed the building from basement to rooftop garden and children's playground." There seemed to be something for everyone, as curious patrons browsed the sales floors, viewing merchandise and floral displays while listening to live music.

After the opening, the store weathered six months of poor sales due to a citywide recession. Business improved in the ensuing years, and the store expanded to meet its ever-growing customer base and the demand for fine products and service. Bullock's Inc. was formed in 1927 to acquire the business and its assets from the estate of Arthur Letts.

John Bullock passed away on September 15, 1933, after suffering a heart attack at his home at 627 South Plymouth Boulevard. In addition to his widow, Bullock left behind two daughters from a former marriage, Margaret S. Bullock and Mrs. Richard William Fewel. Tributes to Bullock poured in from across the city. The *Los Angeles Times* wrote, "Nationally known as one of America's merchant princes, who through purpose, energy and character had from a modest beginning risen to one of the highest positions in the western business world. Mr. Bullock will long be remembered gratefully and affectionately by the people of Southern California for reasons of community service that represented heavy sacrifice of time and energy without personal gain."

The vision for Bullock's was created by Arthur Letts (right), owner of The Broadway Department Store. He assigned his esteemed employee John Bullock (left) the task of creating a more affluent retail establishment to cater to the upper echelon of shoppers.

One

BULLOCK'S
DOWNTOWN

From early in its conception, Bullock's Downtown Los Angeles was more than a department store flagship; it was an integral part of the community. From day one, the store offered quality merchandise and prime customer service to the thousands of people who lived, worked, and shopped downtown.

But Bullock's was more. The store was for many youngsters the first place they received a haircut while sitting on a carousel animal in the barber shop, or where they experienced the fun of sliding down the storybook-inspired Playland slide that connected one Bullock's building with another. From mother to grandmother, women enjoyed shopping at the store and appreciated all the extra perks that were offered. The Galerie de Charme was an exclusive environment where women sought beauty aids for face, hair, and hands. The Tea Room was the meeting place for multiple generations of friends and family. Mother took daughter to lunch and to her first tea room fashion show, and friends would often meet for lunch, fashion shows, or just to catch up. Bullock's Men's Store had what most every man wants: service, selection, and privacy. The store catered to the male taste for decades.

Every working morning in 1907, Bullock's team of seven horses and chocolate brown delivery wagons would line up on Seventh Street for inspection. Each wagon was clean of dirt and brightly polished. The horses were well groomed, with teeth cleaned of hay. The seven wagons would begin a single-file march around the block, as if in a parade. This Bullock's parade would continue as the store served the Los Angeles community.

One example of this service was Bullock's offering its customers and staff a lending library. The store was famous for its countless free exhibits and displays on local artists and designers, as well as reports from around the world on subjects like the Panama Canal in 1914 and the Olympic games in Los Angeles in 1932.

The store even welcomed healthy competition. When J.W. Robinson's opened its new store on Seventh Street and Grand Avenue, Bullock's and other retailers in the area printed large advertisements in the newspapers welcoming them to the neighborhood. John Bullock and his store also weathered harsh political criticism when William Randolf Hearst took action against the store's bridge over city-owned Saint Vincent Court.

The Broadway store opened on June 28, 1913, and, with a newer, larger building, Letts was able to expand on the department concept even further. Each merchandise type, such as women's, children's, and furniture, was found within its own uniquely decorated selling space. The Broadway always had something happening. Letts felt that part of his key to success was to be a part of the community and to always give back. He had no issue with store promotion and publicity, as long as it was meaningful.

The Broadway store opened on June 28, 1913, and, with the larger building, Letts was able to expand on the department concept even further. Each merchandise type, such as women's, children's, and furniture, was found within its own uniquely decorated selling space. The Broadway always had something happening. Letts felt that part of his key to success was to be a part of the community and to always give back. Letts had no issue with store promotion and publicity, as long as it was meaningful. Here the cast of "The Little Rascals" from Hal Roach's *Our Gang* comedies lace up new Broadway shoes in a promotion to help underprivileged children get new shoes.

The Broadway rooftop Italian Garden, with its spacious café, was located on the top floor. This was a place for customers to take time to enjoy the lush landscaping and sculptures after tea or a meal in the café. Both The Broadway and Bullock's continued this tradition in future stores.

The future site of Bullock's is pictured here around 1905. St. Vincent's College had occupied the site 20 years before; later, these wooden flats lined Seventh Street. Many of these three-story structures were homes and businesses, with the shop or service just above the street and the proprietor living above or behind it. A "Printing Co." sign announces one of the original tenants.

Construction began in early 1906 on a seven-story structure at Seventh Street and Broadway. Owner Edwin T. Earl had ambitious plans for the site, but, unfortunately, he ran out of capital to finish the job. Earl asked Letts if he could take the building. Letts agreed, with the stipulation that he would be charged a low rent.

P.G. Winnett, like Arthur Letts and John Bullock, was a true "merchant prince." Winnett (pictured at right) started with Letts's Broadway store as a cash boy when it opened. His responsibilities included running errands in the store and, in his spare time, stringing shoe buttons for $2 a week. Both Letts and Bullock kept an observant eye on him, as he always did more work than he was supposed to do. In men's furnishings, Winnett was assigned to keep up the sizes of celluloid collars; he eventually became manager of the department. When Bullock was organizing the new Bullock's store, he persuaded Winnett to be his chief assistant, vice president of Bullock's. Winnett would go on to build and operate even grander stores in the Bullock's empire.

This photograph captures Bullock's around January 1, 1907. This was a relatively isolated building at the time Bullock's occupied it. With the exception of the Lankershim Hotel, there were no large structures in the vicinity of Broadway and Seventh Street. It was "too far down Broadway, too far from the retail district," according to Bullock's obituary in the *Los Angeles Times*.

This March 2, 1907, Los Angeles newspaper advertisement— one of the very first for the store—announces Bullock's formal opening. Bullock's was a regular advertiser in Los Angeles newspapers, appearing almost daily. The store opened for business the following Monday, March 4. In a store tradition that continued for many years, female employees dressed in turn-of-the-century costumes and handed out violets to customers on the anniversary of that day.

THE BEST EQUIPPED DEPARTMENT STORE IN THE WEST.

The Pioneer Store of the New Shopping Zone

Bullock's
7th & Broadway
Either Phone Exchange 1500

Formal Opening

===TAKES PLACE===

Saturday Night, March 2nd 7:30 to 10 O'CLOCK

No Cards ...... Everybody Cordially Invited ...... Come and Enjoy Yourselves

Entertainment Features	Burbank's World Famous Water Color Drawing
THE HAMMERMEYER ORCHESTRA THE L.A. LETTER CARRIERS BAND Elizabeth Nolle .. The California Mocking Bird HALBERG'S CONCERT ORCHESTRA Ethel Pearl Mitchell .. Solo Cornetist STAMM'S ORCHESTRA Rawson's DOG AND PONY CIRCUS Introducing Sleepy Tom...... The Wonderful Trick Pony	*The* Angel Delivering Daniel Covering 200 Square Feet Valued at $100,000.00 We take great pleasure in presenting to the Los Angeles public this famous picture. As a work of art this picture stands alone—the largest water color in the world, stronger and more durable than oil; being done in stipple, it has a remarkable softness. Having no gloomy associations, it inspires the beholder with the highest conceptions of the poetic and sublime.

Men's Wear	Women's Wear	Children's Wear
Our stock of men's goods includes some of the best makes of ready-to-wear garments known to the clothing trade—notably Garson Meyer & Co.'s Rochester made suits and other lines equally as well known.	Our women's garment section will be one of the beauty spots of this establishment; here will be displayed all that is new and much that is novel in ready-to-wear garments for women.	We will devote a large space on the fourth floor to misses', children's and infants' wear, displaying a most comprehensive line of wearables for the infant, the little girl of 4 to 8 and the miss just budding into womanhood.

First Public Engagement of the L. A. Letter Carriers Band

This c. 1910 photograph captures a street floor view of Bullock's. The main level set the tone and style for what the customer was to expect. From its inception, the store was perceived as offering finer quality merchandise than that found in other Los Angeles stores. This imposing floor, with its high ceilings and ornate décor, was also the perfect setting for cultural, patriotic, and seasonal displays.

The Gown Room was located on the third floor. Each floor in Bullock's was designed with individual sales salons, rooms, or departments. Some were more ornate than others. Oak paneling, lead-glass doors, brightly lit display cases, and an abundance of potted plants lent themselves nicely to the finer selling areas.

Bullock's Tea Room foyer had beautifully appointed furnishings, including imported rugs, wicker chairs, and floral arrangements. Patrons were thus able to enjoy the surroundings while they waited for teatime. Often, the room offered waiting customers live music from string quartets.

The eighth-floor Tea Room and, later, dining room, was a popular feature in the store. Steeped in English and European tradition, the room served traditional tea service along with full luncheon fare. The space also hosted many special presentations, including lectures, readings, and bridge and card instructions. Its daily fashion shows and informal modeling of Bullock's fine fashions were most favored. In February 1957, the space was redecorated, and the name was changed to the Palmetto Room.

This is one of many striking cover designs of the Tea Room menu, created by artists from throughout the Los Angeles area and by Bullock's in-house artists. Many of these covers were printed by the hand-pulled silk-screen method.

In December 1910, Bullock's leased the Hollenbeck Building ("California Furniture Store") on Broadway for $1 million. Only three years after opening, Bullock's saw a record growth in sales, requiring the addition of the former furniture store's 71,000 square feet. This was just the beginning of Bullock's downtown expansion. In 1914, a marble floor was laid for the entire Broadway building.

NEEDLEWORK— FINE EXAMPLES FROM EUROPE

An Italian Crash Linen Luncheon Set, hand embroidered.

No. 3744—18x54 inch Scarf with 12 doylies at $17.50 set.

No. 3745—18x54 inch Scarf with 6 doylies and 6 napkins, at $17.50 set.

No. 3752—Italian Linen Crash Breakfast Set consisting of a 24-inch square em-

The delicate traceries of Real Brittany Laces in a lovely Bed Spread, double bed size, No. 3733, priced at $150.00.
It is presented to direct your thoughts toward Bullock's splendid collection of Laces from Brittany—each piece a personal Bullock selection—each piece a precious example of an art that is centuries old. Other fine double bed size Brittany Lace Bed Spreads at $125.00.

LACES OF THE HEIRLOOM KIND LASTING GIFTS

The outstanding characteristic of Bullock's Art Needlework and Gift Store is expressed in determination to gather together Gifts that are unique.

Personal journeys to foreign shores have resulted in the discovery of much that is rare in old world art—much that is distinctive in its field—particularly applicable to giving—for many occasions the year round.

Rare Italian Filet and Cut work Boudoir Pillow Covers filled with pink, blue or yellow covered pillows.

No. 3748—11x17 pillows at $5.00.

No. 3749—18x22 pillows at $10.00.

Bullock's Linen Room is pictured in the store's 1928 catalog. Among the items displayed is handmade fine linen from northern France.

The sales floor of Bullock's Gown Salon is pictured here. Most early merchandise was imported from Europe, with shirtwaists and undergarments produced locally. For the selection and transport of quality goods to the store, Bullock's operated many offices. Paris and London were the store's European buying offices, along with one in New York. Additional offices were located at the shipping port in San Pedro and the Mercantile Building in downtown Los Angeles.

Bullock's produced advertisements that were commonly seen in Los Angeles–area newspapers, such as the *Los Angeles Times* and the *Herald Examiner*. Glossy West Coast magazines included *California*, *Westways*, and *Sunset*. The store used both photography and illustration in its advertisements, which were often graced by Hollywood motion-picture personalities. Actress Lois Wilson, known for her many roles with Rudolph Valentino, posed for many advertisements.

Bullock's was one Los Angeles establishment that did not overlook the power of outdoor advertising via billboards. While other department stores and shops alerted the passing public of new fashions, Bullock's kept the message simple: "Ideals, Initiative, Hospitality and Imagination."

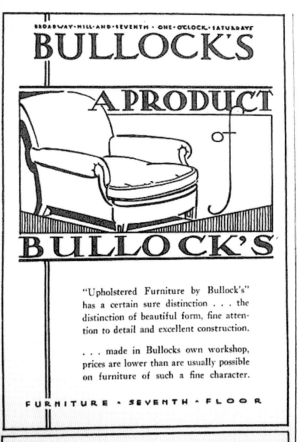

are centers of summer interest. Brook-
side park plunge and the High School
pool attract collegiates from other towns
and make Pasadena a summer watering
place.

ART

LOS ANGELES MUSEUM, Exposition
Park, announces the following exhibi-
tions for the month:
September 1-15, Hanson Puthuff, Conrad
Buff, and Lorser Feitelson and Nathalie
Newking.
September 15-30, paintings by six art-
ists, sent from the State Museum of Ufa,
Russia.

PALACE OF THE LEGION OF HONOR,
San Francisco, will continue to be the
center of art interest in sculpture for
the next several months. The National
Sculpture Society, sponsoring the All-
American Exhibition of Contemporary
Sculpture, has decided to extend the exhibition to the first of the year, continuing also the policy of charging no ad-
mission. The purposes of the exhibition,
as stated by the Society, are "to en-
courage the American artist and to edu-
cate further in artistic standards the
American public."

HENRY E. HUNTINGTON ART GAL-
LERY, San Marino, California, will remain closed during September. Two
new wings are planned, construction of
which will almost double the library
capacity and make possible the exhibition of many choice manuscripts, books,
and art treasures.

CUMP GALLERIES, 268 Post Street, San
Francisco, offer a general exhibition of
paintings, a well selected group by well
known artists. In the Print Rooms the
work of European and American etchers
is shown.

JOSE DRUDIS-BIADA held an exhibition
of paintings in the galleries of the Art
League of Santa Barbara, California,
last month.

LAGUNA BEACH ART ASSOCIATION,
Laguna Beach, California, added to the
building fund through an auction sale
of small paintings donated by artist
members, no canvas exceeding seven by
nine inches. Many delightful pictures
were contributed and changed hands.

TWENTY-EIGHTH INTERNATIONAL
EXHIBITION OF THE CARNEGIE IN-
SCITUTE of Pittsburg opens October
17 and continues through December 8.
In addition to the usual Carnegie prizes
and that offered by the Garden Club of
Allegheny County, there will be awarded
this year for the first time the Albert

From 1929, Bullock's was proud to have its own furniture workshops custom creating handsome designs. The store also sold world-renowned furniture designs from Lincoln-Orinoco.

This Bullock's December 1910 advertisement features Santa Claus opening up the roof of the store, which is laden with gifts for everyone. For merchandisers, Christmas is very important to annual sales. The store, aware of the importance of children, had a circus-themed barbershop and a toyland slide.

The bargain basement was a staple in almost every department store in the nation. The basement was a whole store itself, offering a full range of goods at affordable prices. Bullock's Bargain Basement featured an informal café with an open kitchen, where a very tasty soup of the day simmered in a huge copper kettle.

Known as "The Flying Squadron," these young women were relief exchange clerks, cashiers, inspectors, and female floorwalkers. Not only did these up-and-coming women provide lunch and break reliefs in the store, they also assisted with any distress calls. Both Bullock and Winnett believed strongly in hiring employees with integrity and standards. Bullock's was proud to employ people of all backgrounds, cultures, and faiths.

When Walt Disney's Mickey Mouse made Americans laugh at the movies, Disney set out to produce merchandise of the mouse as well. Charlotte Clark, a maker of handmade dolls, created the very first Mickey Mouse doll. Clark and her small staff produced each one, and they were first sold exclusively at Bullock's.

This is an early Bullock's *Book of Gifts* mail-order catalog from 1928. This store-produced, multi-page catalog presented the best Bullock's had to offer to its select customers. Fine china, silver, rare books, and antiques were just a few of the offerings. The brilliant cover design was also utilized by the store in gift boxes, wrapping paper, and seasonal correspondence.

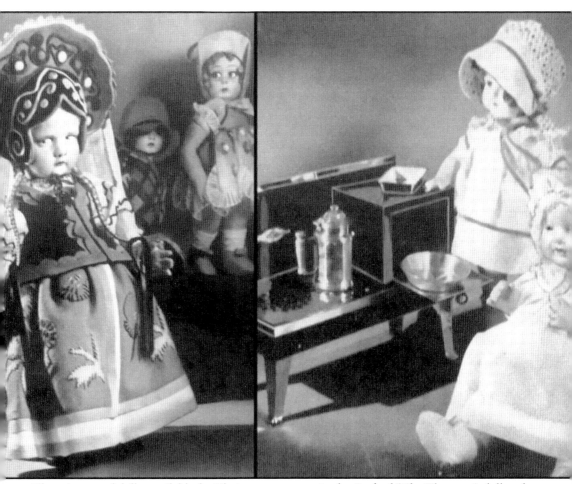

These imported dolls, available for Christmas, are seen in the *Book of Gifts*. The store's doll and toy assortment was vast, featuring everything from fine porcelain figures from Italy in traditional dress to sunbonnet babies made of composition and produced locally. The catalog states, "Think of Bullock's as Santa's agent in Los Angeles."

Here, a 1920s window display featuring a spring wedding theme dazzles customers. The downtown department store would not be a department store without beautifully designed windows. Bullock's was no exception, allotting its display department a large budget, an educated staff, and the freedom to create the most vibrant and unique displays.

Windows and in-store displays were changed regularly. Raymond Dexter was head of this department for many years. He and his staff were kept informed on what Bullock's would be promoting six or more months ahead. Designs were first presented, then approved by Winnett before they were created and installed. Employees often worked long hours with the windows covered from view. The unveilings were always hailed with applause. Dexter had a long career with the store, designing many of the later branch stores.

"One O'clock Saturdays" is often mentioned in advertisements from the 1920s and 1930s. John Bullock believed his staff worked hard and deserved a life outside of the store. Bullock's was open from 8:00 a.m. to 1:00 p.m. on Saturdays, so that the staff could enjoy time off. The store kept regular weekday hours and was closed on Sundays.

What better place to showcase fashions and sportswear than on the store's rooftop garden? Throughout the 1920s and 1930s, the sportswear department was one of the highest-grossing departments in terms of sales. Sunny California lent itself to the active outdoors lifestyle, with clientele partaking in tennis, golf, and shuffleboard. Equestrian sports, such as riding and polo, were also very popular; the store added a Saddle Shop to outfit any rider.

By 1924, the delivery department had grown from seven one-horse wagons to thirty-one delivery cars and three motorcycles. The department expanded to the street level of the store's Stanford Avenue service building, which covered over 57,000 square feet. This building functioned as a delivery service hub and as workrooms for the production of drapery, carpet, and furniture. The building was designed by John and Donald Parkinson.

Bullock's was a full-service department store that offered unprecedented services for its patrons. Planning a visit to the Louvre? An evening at the opera? Dinner reservations? Bullock's concierge could handle it all.

John Bullock took great pride in his adopted country. He believed in offering his customers the best in everything, from exotic imports to custom-made American merchandise. The American Way was one department dedicated to US-created designs for the home.

Seen here is the entrance of the Men's Store on Hill Street. Traditionally, men prefer to shop by themselves. Even in the 1930s, it was uncommon to see a whole family on a day out shopping, so stores began making special conveniences for their male customers. Initially, stores featured men-only entrances, but soon, whole stores were dedicated to the male shopper and his lifestyle. An all-male staff provided assistance in the Smoking Room, the most popular.

The Men's Store was unique in its design and layout. The addition, built by favored architects John and Donald Parkinson, featured a clean, streamlined facade. The main floor's walls, lighting, and display cases were designed in varying geometric sizes. The overall effect produced an Art Deco feel.

This mural adorned the walls of the Men's Store. The striking fresco by Millard Sheets depicted the growing of cotton and spinning machinery, along with working tailors in the act of sewing garments. The mural was nine feet wide by sixteen feet high.

Los Angeles is famous for its automobile traffic. While most people came to work and shop in downtown by car, others chose to take the city's streetcars and buses. Bullock's made sure its customers were riding the right transportation and routes, placing advertisements on the sides and fronts of the vehicles. In the 1940s and 1950s, 80 percent of the city's transit yellow line passed by Bullock's.

The living room department was more exhibit than sales area. Bullock's was a trendsetter in the presentation and promotion of foreign and domestic furniture, decorative art, and accessory home goods. From a one-of-a-kind "made in France" vase to hand-tooled copper ware produced by a Los Angeles–based artist, Bullock's always had unique and interesting goods displayed. Some local artists would go on to produce merchandise for the store and even contribute to the interior design of Bullocks Wilshire.

This is a bedroom display from the 1930s. Most items were one-of-a-kind and had to be special ordered from the artist or manufacturer. Bullock's made sure that any item the store presented was of superior quality and delivered to the customer in a timely fashion.

Following World War II, servicemen returned home to Southern California and Los Angeles. For the newly married, with a new job and a home, Bullock's created a "Home Makers' Service" that would help furnish any size house on any given budget.

This postwar home, located on Wilshire Boulevard at Highland Avenue, was developed by the Fritz B. Burns Research Division for Los Angeles Housing architects Walter Wurdeman and Welton Becket. Bullock's interior design department was responsible for this showcase home's furnishings. Bullock's had furnished, and would continue to furnish, model and display homes in Southern California for many years.

Bullock's
HOME STORE

TUNBRIDGE SHOP

NTIQUITIES for TODAY'S HOME

Collector or no...take time out to visit Bullock's Tunbridge Shop. Enjoy a precious hour in an atmosphere charmed by treasures of 18th century England... furniture and bibelots...as well as choice examples of Americana. A place dreamed up for those who find the beauty of fine old things wine for the spirit. Shop in the Furniture Floor...the Seven...

One of Bullock's ideals was expansion through branch stores. As Los Angeles grew, Bullock's grew with it. The downtown store expanded into several adjoining buildings, and plans were developed for a store on Wilshire Boulevard in the 1920s and, in the early 1930s, a smaller shop in Westwood Village.

The Tunbridge Shop, located adjacent to the furniture department, carried a choice selection of decorative antiques from England and from America's East Coast.

The 1950s and 1960s saw an increase in advertisements for the downtown store in newsprint, magazines, and mailers. During this time, the downtown store and each suburban branch store employed their own buyers and art, display, and marketing departments.

This 1957 catalog reminds shoppers to get "Christmas gifts for them." By the mid-1950s, Bullock's Christmas merchandise selection had grown so massive that the store had to produce and send its customers several eye-catching catalogs before December. The catalogs featured perfumes and lingerie for women, and smoking jackets and leather goods for the men. But the most anticipated catalog of the year was the children's toy and Christmas decor selection.

The alley that Bullock's bridged in its expansion to Hill Street was on the former site of Saint Vincent's School. The first Catholic college in Los Angeles was founded in 1865 in the heart of Chinatown. In 1867, a Mr. O. Childs presented Saint Vincent's with 10 acres of land bordered by Sixth, Seventh, Hill, and Fort (now Broadway). Then, in 1893, the school moved. It is now known as Loyola Marymount University. The original building was torn down, and the land was subdivided. By March 1907, Bullock's department store opened on the site. In 1957, Bullock's was registered as a California Historical Landmark, and a plaque was placed on the structure.

Bullock's Downtown occupied a site on Broadway, Seventh Street, and Hill Street. By 1934, Bullock's had a total of eight buildings, with eight acres of total floor space. Over the ensuing decades, Bullock's would change and remodel the store's many departments. After the downtown store closed its doors in 1983, the building's interior was altered to include a jewelry mart, retail outlets, and parking.

Two

Bullocks Wilshire
The Art Deco Masterpiece

Bullocks Wilshire had always been a store unique unto itself. From its opening in September 1929, it had established its own identity, apart from the Bullock's Downtown department store experience. Its architectural design was like no other retail establishment in the nation. Its interior salons and sales rooms were styled with the utmost care and detail, different than those found in America's large and boxy downtown department stores. The Bullocks Wilshire staff were the best of the best, knowledgeable, well trained, and highly skilled at providing the finest in customer service.

What set Bullocks Wilshire apart from other stores and even the Bullock's Downtown store was that it was a "specialty store." In the 1920s, typical department stores carried everything a customer would ever need, from clothing to food. Most large-scale department stores in the United States boasted 50 to 80 individual departments, hence the name "department store."

Bullocks Wilshire was designed to cater to a select clientele whose discretionary dollars would not be spent in everyman departments such as hardware, notions, or appliances. Bullocks Wilshire was exclusive, and as such, carried only special clothing, jewelry, accessories, perfumes, stationery, small furnishings, and gifts.

The specialty store concept was not new. Neiman Marcus in Dallas, Bergdorf Goodman in New York, and I. Magnin in San Francisco had success with this concept for many years. Los Angeles now had its very own specialty store, but one that was very different from all the rest.

Bullocks Wilshire, conceived by Bullock's vice president and cofounder P.G. Winnett, was seen as an extraordinary retail venture. It was one of the first suburban stores in the country. Most importantly, Bullocks Wilshire was an architectural masterpiece unique to Los Angeles or anywhere in the country. Winnett had traveled to Paris and was influenced by the Art Deco, Modernist, and Bauhaus movements. He assembled an eclectic and very talented group to help realize a grand Bullock's store. English architect John Parkinson and son Donald were enlisted as the lead architects, with Jock Peters of the firm Feil and Paradise and Eleanor LeMarie as principal interior designers. LeMarie, a New York designer, had previously redecorated the downtown store in 1926. She was responsible for hiring 13 artists and designers to collaborate on the store's interior. Salons and departments were designed to be cohesive while retaining some individualism.

Bullocks Wilshire was also special in how employees were to interact with the store's patrons. Employees were to say "we," not "I," "approve," never "OK," and the parking lot was always "the motor court." Employees were to be patient, always standing aside to allow the patron to pass first and giving directions graciously within the store or to another store.

The Irene Salon was dedicated to fashion designer Irene Lentz-Gibbons. Her designs in the 1930s were hailed as "California Fresh" in the press. It was reputed to be the first boutique devoted to a single designer inside a major US store. Lentz designed custom wardrobes for celebrities, leading to a career in design at major film studios, including MGM. Movie stars needed to have originals custom made by her. Greer Garson, Ginger Rogers, Dolores Del Rio, Vivian Leigh, and the Hancock Park old wealth of Los Angeles all wore Irene.

Hollywood soon discovered the store. Screen stars Marion Davies and Mae West were regulars. Scenes for the Cary Grant film *Topper* were filmed at the porte cochere, and the 1969 Bing Crosby *Christmas Special* was shot there. The daytime drama *General Hospital* had favorite characters Luke and Laura locked in the store overnight. Some celebrities even worked there. Angela Lansbury and June Lockhart were employed at the store, and author Helen Gurley Brown worked as a secretary. The store even helped Hollywood celebrate its centennial with an inflatable King Kong on its tower.

The store weathered the Great Depression, World War II, and changing patron demographics. In 1990, owner R.H. Macy decided to retire the Bullocks Wilshire nameplate in favor of I. Magnin. The Wilshire store and six branch stores were renamed. After extensive damage and looting on the first floor during the Los Angeles riots of 1992, the store shut its doors for good in 1993. All the remaining I. Magnin and former Bullocks Wilshire branch stores were closed by January 1995.

Bullocks Wilshire opened on September 24, 1929. The five-story, terra-cotta and copper-faced structure was built within raised setbacks. Its striking tower rises 241 feet above Wilshire Boulevard. (Courtesy of the Richard M. Martinez collection.)

The car entrance off Wilshire Place included bronze gates in a stylized sunburst design. Bullocks Wilshire was one of the first stores to acknowledge the growing use of the automobile. The store provided an ample parking area behind the building, with an equally grand entrance. (Courtesy of the Richard M. Martinez collection.)

Patrons were greeted by friendly valet attendants and doormen at the porte cochere, or automobile entrance. The mural overhead was the work of artist Herman Sachs. Titled *Speed of Transportation*, it colorfully depicted various forms of transport, including the automobile, by which patrons arrived. (Courtesy of the Richard M. Martinez collection.)

Featured about the doors of the Wilshire Boulevard street entrance is a relief by artist George Stanley, the man who created the original Academy Awards Oscar statuette. The bas-relief panel features stylized human figures and John Bullock's motto: "To build a business that will never know completion." (Courtesy of the Richard M. Martinez collection.)

Perfume Hall, or central hall, was a corridor extending through the store from the street to the rear automobile entrance. The highly polished walls are of St. Genevieve marble quarried in Missouri. The vertical inset lighting is incandescent. The flooring, which continued the zigzag pattern, was of faux marble rubber material, which absorbed and reduced noise. (Courtesy of the Richard M. Martinez collection.)

The doors of the six elevators displayed an abstract Bauhaus design of copper, gunmetal, and bronze. The Bauhaus machinery theme is continued in the central clock on the south wall, over the automobile entrance. (Courtesy of the Richard M. Martinez collection.)

When visiting the perfume and skin department, patrons were asked to have a seat while staff waited on them. Employees were encouraged to establish a personal rapport with clients and to know their names and preferences. Black books were issued to staff for patron information, including name, contact information, previous purchases, interests, and any special requests. (Courtesy of the Richard M. Martinez collection.)

The accessories alcove was found east of the elevator lobby. This large department was originally decorated in hues of tan, pink, and robin's-egg blue. The central and largest part of the area was a semicircular seating section in the shoe department. Lighting for this grand room was originally provided by a series of custom-made tubular glass chandeliers. (Courtesy of the Richard M. Martinez collection.)

For years, Bullock's Downtown had tremendous sales growth in sportswear. Designed by Jock Peters, the room was warm and inviting with an overall feeling of the "California Lifestyle." The mural *The Spirit of Sports* was by artist Gjura Stojano. (Courtesy of the Richard M. Martinez collection.)

Jock Peters's design for the Men's shop is seen here. The drawing shows Peters's use of horizontal and vertical lines for this department.

The Wilshire Street entrance of the Saddle Shop is captured here. When the store opened, the shop had "Bullock's Barney," a life-size plaster horse that patrons could mount in order for a tailor to check the fit of their riding breeches. (Courtesy of the Richard M. Martinez collection.)

The Saddle Shop's ceiling was a blue and grey checkerboard pattern with chalk white walls and a brick floor covered in Navajo rugs. A plaster relief titled *The Hunt*, by artist Eugene Maier-Krieg, a German immigrant, showed polo players along with deer and other wildlife. The artist also was responsible for the terra-cotta bas-relief over the entrance of the Title Guarantee and Trust Building at Fifth and Hill Streets. (Courtesy of the Richard M. Martinez collection.)

This show window was created by Jock Peters. Window displays were the eyes into the store, enticing the casual passerby and giving birth to the practice of window shopping. A talented team of designers and craftsmen worked together behind the scenes to produce these complex scenes over the years, and Bullock's use of window space set a high precedent for future installations.

Angela Lansbury was hired by Bullocks Wilshire in December 1942 as a cashier and returned after the holidays working in cosmetics because of her beautiful alabaster skin. She left the store in June 1943 after a successful screen test with MGM Studios. (Courtesy Library of Congress.)

The second-level
Louis XVI Room or
"Louis Seize Room,"
was the setting
for finer apparel.
Done in ivory
and antique gold,
the salon was an
interpretation of Marie
Antoinette's boudoir
at Versailles.
(Courtesy of
the Richard M.
Martinez collection.)

The other "period" room located on the second level was the Directoire. Decorated by George De Winter, the room displayed copies of *The Monuments of Paris*. The faux fireplace and mantle were finished in a rich mahogany. The fine apparel salons originally excluded display mannequins and racks, as garments were displayed for the patron by a house model. (Courtesy of the Richard M. Martinez collection.)

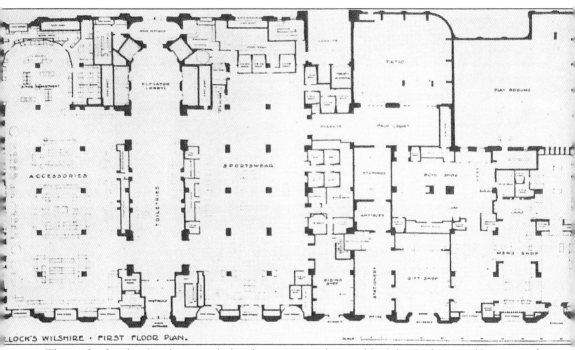

This is the first-level architectural plan from 1929, as designed by John Parkinson. (Courtesy of the Richard M. Martinez collection.)

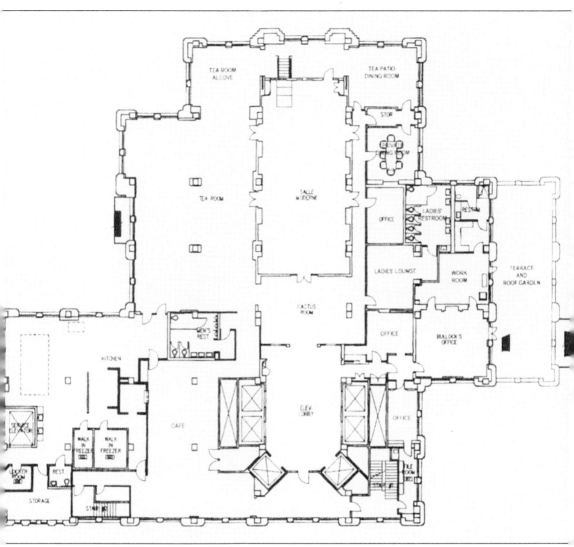

Architectural plans for the fifth level show the Cactus Room, Salle Moderne, and the Tea Room, as well as kitchen facilities. In the late 1940s, both the Cactus Room and Salle Modern were remodeled. By the 1960s, the Tea Room had undergone renovation. This floor also housed John Bullock's private office and a garden terrace overlooking downtown Los Angeles. (Courtesy of the Richard M. Martinez collection.)

The beauty parlor, or Studio of Beauty's Swirl Room, was designed by Jack Weber and Eleanor LeMarie. Originally, the salon had 18 stations and a black-and-white decor. The flooring and visible plumbing fixtures were of a synthetic marble material. (Courtesy of the Richard M. Martinez collection.)

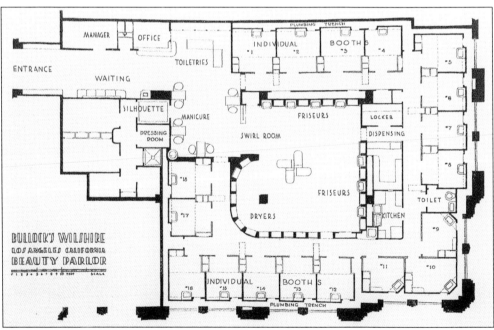

The beauty parlor was fully equipped. Eleanor LeMarie was one of the first female commercial interior designers. One of Stanley Marcus's favorite designers, LeMarie not only did work for Bullock's, but planned many of Neiman Marcus's early branch stores. (Courtesy of the Richard M. Martinez collection.)

This is a view into the Cactus Lounge, situated on the fifth level. Designed by John Weber, it was decorated in a Southwestern palette of soothing greens, yellows, and browns. The illuminated glass ceiling was designed by Herman Sachs. (Courtesy of the Richard M. Martinez collection.)

This photograph was taken after the 1940s remodeling of the elevator lobby on the fifth level. In 1969, the store was the first on the West Coast to introduce the French ready-to-wear collections of Hubert de Givenchy and Phillippe Venet. Most of the second floor was remodeled into a white-and-chrome duplicate of Givenchy's Avenue Victor Hugo boutique in Paris. (Courtesy of the Richard M. Martinez collection.)

The store was the place to go for fashion and fragrance before an evening at the opera, a motion-picture premiere, or a high-society affair. Bullocks Wilshire's patrons were always the best-dressed attendees.

This Los Angeles newspaper advertisement promotes the ease of automobile access to Bullocks Wilshire. The store's location outside of traffic-congested downtown made driving to the store as enjoyable as shopping there.

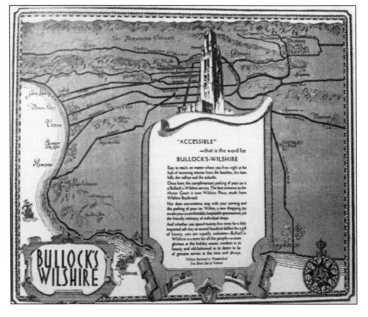

This announcement recognizes the store's volunteer involvement in the Los Angeles community. Bullocks Wilshire was host to countless in-store fundraisers and charitable events.

The Junior League
of Los Angeles
announces
"Bullock's-Wilshire Day"
Wednesday, November 5th, 1930

Which means that the Junior League of Los Angeles has arranged to take over the activities of the store co-operatively with bullock's-wilshire for that day, in the interest of Junior League activities and charities.

This is the first venture of this kind in Los Angeles and the League solicits the patronage of its members and friends that the fund may be the larger from the effort.

Junior League Members
Will Act, For the Day, as
Manikins
Saleswomen
Hostesses
Stylists
Decorators
    in every section of
    the store—come!

BULLOCK'S
WILSHIRE

Wilshire Boulevard
at Westmoreland

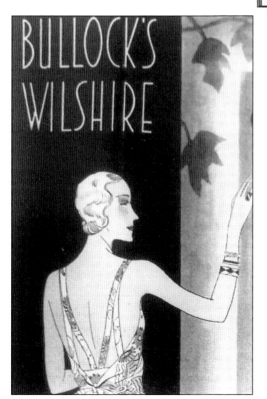

Most of the store's advertising was done locally through the newspaper. However, occasionally, select black-and-white advertisements could be found in glossy national magazines and publications.

John Bullock's daughter Margaret opened a small flower shop at the corner of Wilshire Boulevard and Wilshire Place, next to the imposing Wilshire store. Bullock's itself did not sell fresh flowers, but his daughter's shop aided patrons with their purchases of fashion and flowers. (Courtesy of the Richard M. Martinez collection.)

The flower shop was designed and decorated by the store's own stylist, Raymond Dexter. Even though Margaret's Flowers was not directly affiliated with the Bullock's corporation, the shop was part of the family. Morgan, Walls & Clements were the shop's architects. (Courtesy of the Richard M. Martinez collection.)

A Christmas tree stands in the elevator lobby on the first floor. For years, the store decorated for the season tastefully and elegantly. Most of the trees used on the floor were artificial; early ones were made of glass beads and white pompoms (pictured). A tree and wreaths of pure white feathers adorned the store throughout the 1980s. (Courtesy of the Richard M. Martinez collection.)

The Bullock's and Bullocks Wilshire chains were purchased by Macy's in 1988. Bullocks Wilshire became part of the I. Magnin chain.

BULLOCK'S WILSHIRE

On October 10, 1969, Bullocks Wilshire was declared the city of Los Angeles's 56th Historical and Cultural Monument. On May 25, 1978, the building was honored by being listed in the National Register of Historic Places. In 1994, it was purchased by Southwestern Law School and has been restored to its 1929 look. It now serves as a private school and is no longer open to the public.

The 50th-anniversary catalog (1929–1979), labeled "A Legend Still," offered patrons 50 pages of unique items as only Bullocks Wilshire could provide. Steuben, Daum, Royal Copenhagen, Buccellati, Albert Nipon, Chloe, John Anthony, and Bill Blass were just a few of the exclusives. In 1983, Bullocks Wilshire established a national mail-order catalog business under the name *Invitation*.

Three

BULLOCK'S PASADENA
THE STORE OF THE FUTURE

In early 1945, with World War II winding down, Bullock's was the first California department store to announce that it would be opening a major suburban branch. America's involvement in the war caused great sacrifice across the nation, as the consumption of gasoline, food, and other common necessities was restricted. Nearly all nonessential products were placed on hold, as materials used in new construction were relegated to the war effort.

The Bullock's Pasadena store had been in the planning stages before the war. With an end in hostilities approaching, the company felt it was time to move forward. The "store of the future," as the press would later dub it, was outside of the central Pasadena business district, just like the Wilshire Boulevard location was 18 years earlier. At the time, Pasadena was still considered a small town, but it encompassed a lively business and retail core along its main street, Colorado Boulevard.

The store was created to serve the people of Pasadena and other communities east of Los Angeles. Bullock's number-one objective was always "to serve completely." In order to do so, extreme care was given to every detail, including architecture, interior design, and operation. The location of 401 South Lake Avenue for the building was chosen for several reasons, including South Lake Avenue's easy accessibility from the main highways to outlying areas. The location also offered a large parcel of land on which to build a store befitting the community. With the purchase and removal of over 40 homes, the eight-acre site would eventually hold a three-level, 289,225-square-foot structure with dual parking lots flanking its north and south sides.

Walter Wurdeman and Welton Becket were chosen as the lead architects. This would be both men's first big retail project. Wurdeman and Becket hailed from Seattle, and both graduated from the University of Washington. From the early 1930s, the team had been known as designers for many estates in Hollywood and Beverly Hills, including for Hollywood's motion-picture royalty. Much of their early work was inspired by English, European, and East Coast buildings. In 1934, the group of Plummer, Wurdeman and Becket built one of Los Angeles's most unique icons, The Pan Pacific Auditorium. The auditorium was considered one of the finest examples of Streamline Modern architecture in the United States, and was acknowledged in 1947 with an Honor Award from the Southern California chapter of the AIA.

Walter Wurdeman passed away in 1949, leaving Becket to carry on and start Welton Becket and Associates. Becket's firm would create numerous projects worldwide, including The Beverly

Hilton Hotel (1952), The Capitol Records Building (1955), and Walt Disney World's Contemporary Resort (1971).

In the research and designing of Bullock's Pasadena, Wurdeman and Becket spent almost a year studying every operation and aspect of the Bullock's stores. By talking with customers and store employees, the team learned how the store functioned, what customers bought, and where it was bought in the store. All this research produced a better-running, more-efficient department store. From its opening, Bullock's Pasadena received much praise and many awards from the architectural community. In 1950, the building was given a national AIA Honor Award. Becket would not only design stores again for Bullock's, but for many retail legends across the country, including Marshall Field's, Saks Fifth Avenue, Carson Pirie Scott, Macy's, and I. Magnin.

The building's design called for a low, streamlined, late-modern style, with the southern part in a rectangular shape. The northern side would be more curved, with an upper-level, open terrace. The natural grade of the ground, as well as the preexisting suburban neighborhood, lent themselves to this design. The middle exterior level, mostly visible from the street, would be clad in Pennsylvania fieldstone. The stone was laid by Eastern stonemasons to give it a rough, natural look.

Bullock's Pasadena would have more landscaping than any previous Bullock's store. Its suburban setting and the company's commitment to reflect the indoor-outdoor California lifestyle required the grounds to be well planned and maintained. Pasadena landscape architect Ruth Shellhorn was hired to create a tropical theme. Knowledgeable of the local climate, she carefully selected trees, shrubs, and flowers appropriate for the setting. The placement and size of the trees were such so as to not overwhelm the scale of the building's architecture. Different varieties of palms, lemon gum, and eucalyptus trees provided height and framing. Red hibiscus, used sparingly, added stimulating color, with Carolina jasmine producing a winter gold. Low, sweeping ground covers of ivy and star jasmine provided a textural element to the overall scheme.

Bullock's Pasadena was built for the future. It was dedicated to anticipating the needs of residents by supplying their every demand for merchandise. The Lake Avenue location was mostly residential; almost 50 homes were removed to make way for the new store.

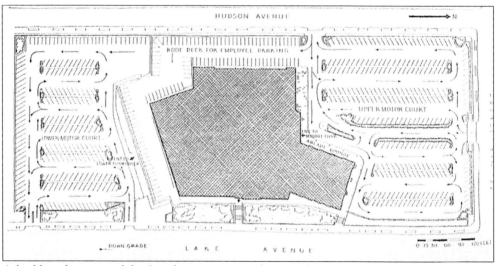

A building footprint of the Pasadena site is seen here, with surface parking on the north and south sides of the store providing 600 spots for enhanced accessibility. Most of the landscaping would face Lake Avenue on the eastern side. In September 1957, a parking garage was added to the south parking area, increasing the number of spaces to 1,500. The store was a destination shopping center completely surrounded by parking.

Bullock's was well known for its many postcards over the years. The Pasadena store was featured on more than 40 cards.

The press described the finished building as more closely resembling a club than a retail store. Local newspapers were quick to assume that the store's appearance and suburban location would result in the venture's total failure. But Bullock's deliberate design vision would successfully attract Pasadena's carriage trade.

The Del Mar Boulevard automobile entrance and parking area provided an indelible service to patrons, creating the ultimate shopping experience. The main entrance was located on the middle level, featuring a large carport and a patio filled with comfortable furniture for customers.

Shown here is the rear of the store, facing west on Hudson Avenue. The building's design was spectacular. Here, the upper-floor windows of the notions department can be seen, along with the rooftop penthouse.

The Toiletries Gallery was housed on the middle level. This long and high-ceilinged space gave visitors quite a first impression. Awash with indirect lighting, the room is bordered in walls of Brazilian rosewood. Lining the hall are small wood-framed cases and counters, designed for displaying a single perfume bottle. Continuing down its full length and covering both sides of the gallery were the store's main murals. Created by Los Angeles artist and Bullock's protégé Annette Honeywell, the murals embraced the store's outdoorsy theme.

Women's sportswear and active sports were also found on the middle level. Floor-to-ceiling windows let in daytime light while overlooking lush landscaping and Lake Avenue.

Georgia Bullock was a saleswoman for the May Company and for Bullock's. She started creating her own designs, which in turn gained national attention. Some of her spring 1962 line for Bullock's Pasadena is pictured here. Georgia Bullock was not known to be related to the John G. Bullock family. (Courtesy of the Pasadena City Directory.)

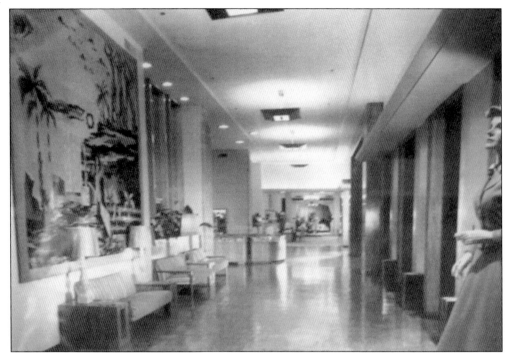

The aim in Pasadena was to create and maintain a community store, suburban in spirit, friendly, and stocked with the finest selection of merchandise.

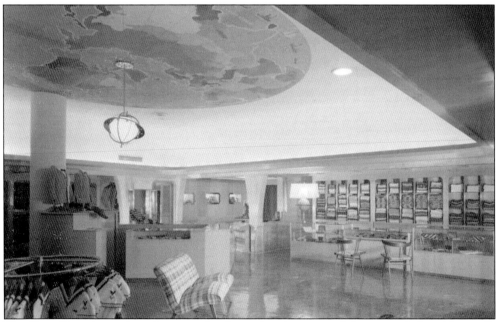

The Boys Shop, located on the upper level, employed a nautical theme, including blue walls accented with natural pine paneling. A balustrade resembling one on an old-time clipper encircles the room. Wall display cases are shaped like portholes and anchors, and rope riggings add to the room's character. Dramatically overhead is a mural of the world by artist Robert Majors, with far-off ports of call where imaginative young boys might dream of sailing.

The Victorian Room, to the right of the toiletries, blended several salon boutiques into one. The main room was dedicated to better clothes, with surrounding shops for furs, hats, shoes, hosiery, and blouses. The room's theme of modern Victorian elegance was selected to honor Pasadena's own Victorian tradition. This room, inspired by a lighter French version, was saturated in soft pinks and blues. Huge faux windows bringing in "outside" light were draped with blue satin damask draperies. Overhead hung two large antique chandeliers of blue Venetian glass.

With the exception of a stairwell, the only way to reach each of the three floors was by unmanned, automatic elevators. Above each of the four mahogany-framed elevators, delicately created back-painted antique mirrors were displayed. These designs, different on each floor, were inspired from Annette Honeywell's portfolio. Directly across from the elevators stood a unique feature of the store's display. A series of floor-to-ceiling wood columns supported panels of plate glass between them. Centered within each glass plate were shadow boxes in grey birch. The individual display boxes appear as if suspended in air.

The Fountain Court, on the lower level, was the central point of the entire Home Store. Circular in design, the court was a place to relax, meet with family members, or just enjoy the calm, cooling fountain. It was a lounge where customers could talk with a salesperson over decorative or design plans. The white chandelier and lacy iron fretwork were quaint reminders of the charm of old New Orleans.

Over the years, this area would be appropriately decorated for Christmas, with a beautiful tree and visits from the store's very own Santa Claus. Coins thrown in the fountain were gathered for local charities. (Courtesy of the Pasadena City Directory.)

The Modern Studio was clean and uncluttered, so as not to distract from the modern furniture itself. One focal point of this room, as in a real home, was a built-in fireplace. It was made of thin, long bricks linked together with a textured mortar. It was sealed and hooded with solid brass accents.

To the right was the open and airy Sun Shop. With two exterior walls of glass, this shop was intended to display patio and outdoor furniture. Expansive wooden dividers, along with the windows, gave an open-air ambiance. All of the woodwork was custom crafted and installed by Los Angeles–based Standard Cabinet Works Inc.

Just behind the Fountain Court, decorative accessories and gifts were housed within a galleria with custom-built maple cabinets and display cases. A low ceiling focused direct lighting on select fine porcelain and crystal objects. Floor-to-ceiling glass cases filled the room, making it visible from the Music Shop, the drapes and curtains department, the Sleep and Boudoir Shop, and the lower elevator foyer.

The Delicacy Shop was a popular department on the lower level. A fine presentation of gift food packages and sweets were offered for all occasions, with hostess gifts being emphasized. California fruits, preserves, jellies, and fancy condiments were most favored.

The Men's Store, located just off the Del Mar Boulevard entrance, offered a comprehensive selection of men's clothing, suits, and accessories. The ceiling was done in light oak, and the floor was composed of red brick. Displayed overhead was a large, opaque watercolor mural depicting the history of Pasadena, by artist Willing Howard.

The lingerie department was situated on the upper level. Also on this floor was a large, sunlit room housing the fabric, sewing, and notions department for clients interested in dressmaking and handiwork. An expansive wall of windows facing west offered the shopper access to natural light to enhance the selection of fabric colors and swatches.

Collegienne, or College Girls, was placed away from the younger shops. Its clientele were not quite ready for the mature Victorian Room on the middle level, so College Girls was a perfect in-between department. The shop featured merchandise for women from junior level to college, and its entrance held display platforms with turned wood posts. Specially designed wallpaper, "Crown City Rose," was a salute to the city of Pasadena by Annette Honeywell. It covered the ceiling back to the millinery. The feel of the Collegienne was of many shops for a young woman arranged close together to create a complete shopping center.

The Coral Room, located on the upper level, was Bullock's Pasadena's very own restaurant. The name came from the store's tropical theme, which was used extensively throughout the tearoom. Annette Honeywell's artistic hand is evident everywhere; her brightly colored and richly detailed murals dominate the space. The same tropical motif is also reflected on the menus, china service, linens, match covers, and even the specially woven carpet. East Indian rosewood was used throughout to complement the murals. Tables and chairs of handcrafted rattan were designed by Paul Laszlo.

One of Bullock's longstanding traditions was its tearoom and luncheon fashion shows. Formal and informal modelings of the latest designs were a daily afternoon occurrence. For large groups, the adjoining Banquet Room could be used as an auditorium for events, lectures, and fashion shows. A large outdoor patio provided al fresco dining on beautiful days.

The Coral Room
Tea Menu

Served Daily (except Monday) from 2:30 to 4:30 P.M.

Suggestions

Fresh shrimp cocktail, 1.00   Fresh crabmeat cocktail, 1.00
Fruit cup, .40
Creamed chicken in pastry shell, jellied salad, spiced
fruit and blueberry muffins, 1.50
Assorted tea sandwiches and fruit cup topped with sherbet. Tea or coffee, 1.25
Pineapple and cottage cheese salad with nut bread, 1.25

Sandwiches

Assorted tea sandwiches, .60   Deviled egg, .60   Chicken salad, .85
Cold baked ham, .85   Tuna salad, .80   Swiss cheese, .65
Cream cheese and jelly on nut bread, .80
Sliced chicken, 1.00   Lettuce and tomato, .65
Avocado and bacon, 1.00

Salads

Chicken, 1.85   Seafood, 1.95   Half avocado filled with seafood, 2.25
Coral Room fruit salad plate with orange nut bread or muffins, 1.75

Breads

Toasted English muffin with preserves, .25
Cinnamon Toast .25; with orange marmalade, .40
Orange nut bread, .25   Pimiento cheese bread, .25   Blueberry muffins, .25
Date nut bread, .25

Desserts

Meringue Shell with ice cream and chocolate sauce or fresh strawberries, .60
Coral Room toasted almond cheese cake, .35   Ice cream or sherbet, .30
Cake, .30; a la mode, .50; Chilled Melon, .30; Pie or tart, .30; a la mode, .50
Fresh pineapple, .40
Raspberry, butterscotch, pineapple or hot fudge sundae, .50
Ice Cream Cake with special Coral Room hot fudge sauce and almonds, .50
Coral Sundae, .50   Pecan ice cream roll, .30   Fruit Jello, .25
Ice box cookies, .25
Cantaloupe a la mode, .60   Fresh strawberry shortcake or sundae, .60

Beverages

Pot of tea or coffee, .25   Buttermilk or milk, .25
Iced tea, .25   Malted milk or milk shake, .50 (made with fresh fruit, .60)
Coca-Cola, .25   Pineapple, orange, grapefruit, or tomato juice, .20
Lemonade, limeade or orangeade, .35   Frosted orange, .55
Ice cream soda, .40 (made with fresh fruit, .50)

(Minimum service twenty-five cents per person)
Daily Fashion Showing

The menu offered a small variety of dishes, but each was a masterpiece. One of the chief responsibilities for hostesses was to recognize and remember returning guests.

The cover of the children's menu is seen here. On being seated, each guest would be served "Rose Bowl Punch" (California orange juice) as a courtesy of the house.

Breakfast with Santa was a store tradition for more than 25 years. A family breakfast was served, along with a visit from Saint Nick. The jolly old man would stop by every table, often telling youngsters to obey their parents and be good to their siblings. The entertainment included a puppet show by Ron Martin. (Courtesy of Francine Orr of the *Pasadena Star News*.)

Pasadena's Tournament of Roses...

"Around the World with Flowers"

Bullock's Pasadena is proud to be part of a city that through the free will efforts of its citizens... various organizations and surrounding communities gives pleasure to millions by creating a spectacle of beauty which is unequalled throughout the world.

Bullock's
PASADENA

Bullock's Pasadena was involved with the annual New Year's Day Pasadena Tournament of Roses event, sponsoring floats, running advertisements in city and program guides, and outfitting the Rose Queen and her court.

This opening advertisement appeared in the *Pasadena Star News* on September 10, 1947. It lists many of the store's unique benefits.

Bullock's Pasadena celebrated its 40th anniversary on September 10, 1987.

This advertisement features one of the many manufacturers that supplied services for the store. C.W. Stockwell Co. produced unique wallpapers and coverings.

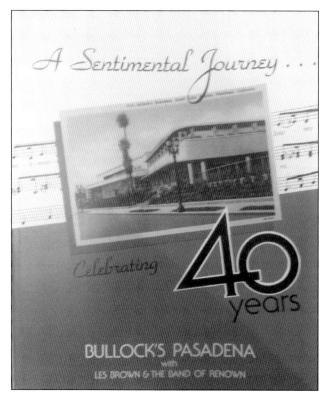

Bullock's/Macy's Pasadena was listed in the National Register of Historic Places on July 12, 1996. This historic placement ensures that the building is deemed worthy of preservation. Pictured here is the cover of the program from the 40th anniversary celebration in 1987.

In 2000, the City of Pasadena permitted some redevelopment on the grounds surrounding the original 1947 structure in order to create The Shops on Lake Avenue, which opened in early 2002. Many felt the close proximity of the new retail space encroached upon the historic Bullock's building. (Courtesy of the Pasadena City Directory.)

Four

BULLOCK'S
FASHION SQUARE
STYLE ARRIVES IN SUBURBIA

The success of the postwar Pasadena Lake Avenue branch proved that the Bullock's ideal could work in outlying suburban areas. However, this store expansion began long before World War II, in rural west Los Angeles. The small store was designed by John and Donald B. Parkinson in Westwood Village near the University of California–Los Angeles. UCLA had allied with the planned retail development from the early 1930s, with the store at Westwood Boulevard and Weyburn Avenue remodeled and expanded several times. Harold Janss, son-in-law of The Broadway founder Arthur Letts, developed the Westwood property into a "romantic village" of European-inspired architecture. This new village was conceived to serve UCLA's faculty and students, along with the area's growing population. Ralph's Grocery Store, Sears, Desmond's, and various shops, banks, and movie theaters rounded out the village's offerings. The complex may be considered one of the first retail developments in the country. The Janss Company had strict control on what would be built and how the buildings would look in Westwood Village. Bullock's Pasadena was such a draw in itself that it created new additional retail surrounding the store. In the 1950s, the concept of the American shopping center was beginning to take hold as retailers and developers saw the need for an all-in-one place to shop, bank, and serve the people of a new suburban community.

Bullock's Inc. saw this opportunity thrive in what it had created on Pasadena's Lake Avenue starting in 1947. Bullock's and its sister store, I. Magnin, could create retail magic again, this time under Bullock's Inc. ownership and control. Company chairman Walter Candy believed in store expansion and that the company's longtime standards must continue: "We stand for fashion and excelled service," he said. "This is our niche in retailing and we're going to keep it that way."

In 1955, Orange County was mostly an agricultural and undeveloped region, with 21 spread-out cities and towns. A drastic change was imminent as the Interstate 5 freeway was working its way south from Los Angeles. Land developers began replacing citrus groves with ranch and storybook tract homes. Cities along the freeway soon became bedroom communities with the required schools, libraries, churches, supermarkets, and retail establishments. The increase in population boosted Orange County's position from the 11th largest county in California in 1950 to the fifth largest just eight years later.

The opening of Disneyland in July 1955 brought national attention to the area. The October opening of the first major department store, The Broadway Center in Anaheim, started filling the need for shopping outlets. A few years after opening, The Broadway Center had annual sales exceeding $25 million.

Bullock's, seeing an opportunity in this exploding demographic, looked south, beyond the Anaheim Broadway Center and Disneyland, to the centrally located county seat of Santa Ana. Bullock's chose a 45-acre site on North Main Street, just a few blocks from the city's older, traditional downtown.

Bullock's Fashion Square, which opened on September 17, 1958, was to be a significant departure from retail centers anywhere else in the nation. The $20 million project would bring together some of the best names in California retail for the first time, at a 340,000-square-foot, three-level store. (Courtesy of the Santa Ana History Room, Santa Ana Public Library.)

William Pereira and Charles Luckman designed the exterior of the store in rich, textured brick, with the upper levels clad in soft, rose, geometric ceramic tile. Landscaped, open-air atrium entrance courts were featured on the north parking side as well as on the south and west, facing the pedestrian Fashion Square side. In one of the key design elements of the square, the central mall, Arboleda Avenue, led to a specially cast concrete fountain court fronting Bullock's main entrance.

Fashion Square was more than just a shopping center. The beautiful grounds also played host to many community events and displays. Art displays, flower shows, vintage car events, and fashion shows were held at Bullock's and the Fashion Square shops.

Brick and iron entry gates led into Bullock's spacious parking area. The center opened with over 600 parking spaces. By 1978, a multilevel parking garage was added to increase capacity.

The center included more landscaping than any other retail complex in the nation. Bullock's landscape architect Patricia Ruth Shellhorn worked to design a unique layout of stone planters and grounds filled with appropriate trees, shrubs, and flowers. Walkways and open lawns interconnect with block planters filled with seasonal foliage and color to create dramatic areas. Over 400 trees and shrubs were selected and planted on the five acres, including Jacaranda, olive, Brazilian pepper, redwood sequoia, eucalyptus, Canary Island pines, hibiscus, bougainvillea, and miscellaneous succulents. Mahlon E. Arnett of Bullock's explained the reason for so much landscaping: "It is true that we have placed a particular emphasis on landscaping for Fashion Square. There are many reasons for this attention, not the least of which is our feeling that we owe it to the community to provide a commercial development that becomes a community asset for its beauty as well as its economic considerations."

VISIT THE 31 DISTINCTIVE STORES OF BULLOCK'S FASHION SQUARE

Bath Shops	542-0351	Jolly Roger	542-3307
Bullock's Santa Ana	547-7211	Jurgensen's	547-5821
C. H. Baker	542-9197	Leed's	542-9327
Darrell's Dedrick Tux	547-6341	Lester, Ryons & Co.	543-9393
Desmond's	542-3921	Magic Mirror Beauty Salon	547-9328
Draper's	547-6089	Mandel's	547-9910
Dr. S. J. Ring, Optometrist	543-3333	Pickwick	547-2775
Elizabeth Byrnes Imported Fashions	541-8330	Plummer's	547-5473
Guy Livingston Ltd.	547-6345	Security First National Bank	547-5811
House of Harmony	547-5971	See's Candy Shop	543-0318
Hugh J. Lowe & Sons	547-4428	Tho'tful Stop Flowers	ask information
I. Magnin & Co.	547-5911	Van Deusen's Jewelry	542-3911
J. Herbert Hall Jewellers	547-5891	Waltah Clarke's Hawaiian Shop	543-8688
Jaclan's Fashions	542-4425	Wetherby Kayser	543-9293
Joel's	543-6522	Young Maternity Shop	542-8374

General Offices 542-2368

FASHION SQUARE SANTA ANA

SANTA ANA FREEWAY AT MAIN, SANTA ANA
SHOP 9:30 A.M. TO 5:30 P.M. MONDAY THROUGH SATURDAY
EVENING SHOPPING MONDAYS AND FRIDAYS UNTIL 9:30 P.M.

Bullock's was able to select who it wanted as tenants in the center. A 30,000-square-foot I. Magnin would complement Bullock's, along with other retailers that worked so well in Pasadena. J.J. Haggarty, Desmond's, and 30 other businesses rounded out the collection. Fashion Square was entirely devoted to shopping goods—the center would not have a traditional supermarket or drugstore. It was the evolution of the idea for a new kind of shopping center, one that caters to the "shopping goods shopper." The center would uphold a high standard of fashion and service.

BULLOCK'S SANTA ANA

OPENS TOMORROW 9:30 A.M.

SEPTEMBER 17, 1958

This grand-opening advertisement was printed in the *Orange County Register*.

The high standards that Fashion Square looked for in its tenants also applied to the appearance of the center itself. Rather than having conflicting architectural styles of buildings, Fashion Square and its eight individual buildings would have an overall theme of early Spanish, Moorish, Mexican, and early California styles while retaining the larger stores' individual personalities. Bullock's stood dominant, at three stories. I. Magnin, Haggarty, and Desmond's were designed in their own style while fitting within the wide loggias surrounding the individual shops.

The Santa Ana main floor is seen here in 1958. The Fountain Court entrance and Accessory Room on the first floor continued the brick exterior of the building. High walls were painted a dusty rose to blend with the brick. The ceiling and overhead lighting were set within suspended geometric squares, providing enough lighting to blend off every surface. Long, wide entry doors and glass windows let the landscaping outside move inside. Brass door handles were designed in a decorative leaf pattern. The overhead shades were of hand-woven dowels and matchsticks in soft cocoa tones. White floor-to-ceiling abstract ceramic screens divided and set apart the adjoining sales rooms.

THE FIRST FLOOR

After-Five Separates
Aprons, Uniforms and Maternity
Blouses
Circle Room Casual Dresses
Circle Room Coats and Suits
Circle Room Dressy Dresses
Circle Room Women's and Half-Size Dresses
Cosmetic Aisle
Daytime Lingerie
Fashion Accessories
Fashion Boutique
Fashion Jewelry
Fine Jewelry
Foundations
Handbags
Luggage and Small Leather Goods
Men's Furnishings
Men's Sportswear
Men's Suits
Nighttime Lingerie
Robes and Negligees
Sportswear Suits and Coats
Sportswear Dresses
Stationery
Venetian Room Dresses
Venetian Room Furs
Venetian Room Suits and Coats
Women's Active Sportswear
Women's Gloves
Women's Hosiery
Women's Millinery
Women's Shoes
Women's Spectator Sportswear
Wynbrier Shop

THE SECOND FLOOR

Baby and Toddler Shop
Boys' Shop
Bride's Room
Children's Shoes
Collegienne Coats and Suits
Collegienne Dresses
Collegienne Lingerie
Collegienne Shoes
Collegienne Sportswear
Estrella Room
Fabrics
Girls' Shop
Hat Tree
Notions
Patterns
Sabrina Shop (Teen)
Sweet Shop
Three to Six Shop
Toys

THE THIRD FLOOR

Bath and Closet Shop
Beauty Studio
Bedroom Accessories
Contemporary Shop
Decorative Accessories
Dining Accessories
Draperies and Curtains
Floor Covering
Gourmet Shop
Housewares
Music and Home Appliances
Provincial Shop
Sleep Shop
Sun Shop
Traditional Shop

Shown here is Bullock's Santa Ana store directory from 1958.

The Venetian Room was designed as an airy, open room, perfect for high-fashion clothing to be modeled or brought out to customers. No clothing racks were ever found in this salon. The room was lit and enhanced by several light fixtures fabricated on the Isle of Murano near Venice, Italy. The first floor also had a large men's department and a long cosmetics aisle, done in polished walnut with built-in display cases.

The Fur Salon, located off the Venetian Room, continued the "less is more" design. Furs were brought out to the customer.

The Fine Jewelry Salon was located on the first floor. Set in its own private space, the salon provided an intimate setting for the selection of fine jewelry.

The third floor held home furnishings, house wares, furniture, and fine china and silver. Silver was displayed within its own alcove, with inset cases and hand-painted murals. The Bridal Registry and Travel Bureau were located close by.

This stunning mural was located on the third floor. At the time, this was touted as the world's largest pastel painting. It was framed by two huge oak doors from Spain.

As with Bullock's other stores, all of the company's buyers lived locally, so they were in touch with their customers and their needs. The Santa Ana store's large basement was the unseen business core, housing offices, storage, shipping and receiving, packing, unloading, display, employee areas, and a cafeteria.

91

Pictured here is the third floor of Santa Ana, which housed the home and furniture gallery. The center of this vast department featured a basilica ceiling with indirect lighting. Antiques included light fixtures from San Francisco's Nob Hill Estates.

Visit the 31 distinctive stores of

BULLOCK'S FASHION SQUARE

is our middle name!

Shop in a leisurely
atmosphere where interesting
things happen and
service is excellent

BULLOCK'S
FASHION
SQUARE
SANTA ANA

SANTA ANA FREEWAY AT MAIN, SANTA ANA
Mondays through Saturdays, 9:30 to 5:30 Monday and Friday, 9:30 to 9:30

Many advertisements for Bullock's Fashion Square were printed in newspapers and Orange County magazines throughout the 1960s and 1970s.

With Bullock's Fashion Square up and running successfully, the company decided to open another location north of Los Angeles, in the vast and ever-growing San Fernando Valley. In October 1959, Bullock's announced that it would build a 307,000-square-foot building and Fashion Square collection of stores on 29 acres bordered to the north by Riverside Drive, on the south by the Ventura Freeway, on the west by Hazeltine Avenue, and on the east by Woodman Avenue in the city of Sherman Oaks. The property was originally the McKinley Home for Boys.

Bullock's Santa Ana location featured the Estrella Room Peppermill. All of Bullock's fine tearooms had custom designed table service themed to each store. Santa Ana's was the star flower of the Australian eucalyptus tree. Eucalyptus was used as windbreaks for citrus crops in Orange County and surrounding Fashion Square.

The interior of the building represented the rich Spanish heritage of the area, as the store was close to the San Fernando Mission. The large store was laid out in defined enclaves, salons, and boutiques designed and decorated with antiques and objects that reflected early cultural influences in California. Many of the antiques were purchased from the William Randolph Hearst estate. Wide aisles led past individual departments decorated in rich woods, textured masonry, and antique chandeliers. One department even had an indoor fountain court with a functioning water well and lion's heads.

The spacious Encino Room, a tearoom, occupied the fourth floor and was decorated in an English garden setting. The north side of the room featured floor-to-ceiling windows that allowed for natural lighting and provided stunning views of the San Fernando Valley.

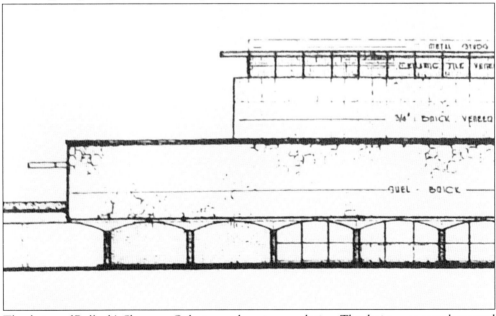

The design of Bullock's Sherman Oaks is seen here in a rendering. The design was complemented with textured brick, split brick, and colorful tiles, which were used on the store's many levels.

The momentum and expansion kept Bullock's moving forward. In March 1964, Bullock's announced to the press that yet another large suburban store was to open in September 1966 in the city of Torrance. The South Bay and Torrance areas were already fully built and well-established communities. May Co. had opened a large store at the South Bay Center in 1959. Farther south down Hawthorn Boulevard in Torrance, The Broadway and Sears had opened in the Del Amo Center in 1959. As with its previous stores, Bullock's felt its store would be a draw in itself—a destination store. Bullock's would not be joining May Co. at South Bay, nor would it join The Broadway at Del Amo. Bullock's was to build its signature Fashion Square concept on land just north of Del Amo.

Bullock's Del Amo, a $10.5 million store, opened on September 12, 1966. Bullock's Del Amo was a four-story structure with a basement, covering almost 256,000 square feet. The split-level building was basically a duplicate of the Lakewood store. Built as two overlapping rectangles in a contemporary design, the building's entrances were located on the first and second floors. The building facade incorporated textured brick, similar to that used for the Valley store.

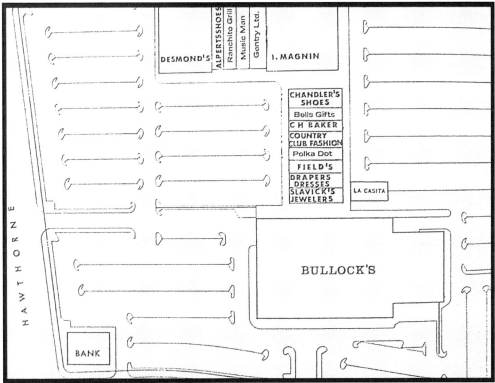

With the established Del Amo Center just across the street, Bullock's decided that this Fashion Square would be smaller than the other two. Bullock's, of course, would be the largest store in the area and would offer its full range of departments and services. The number of individual shops, however, would be limited. Among the 16 stores of distinction were Slavick's, Draper's, Chandler's, Ranchito Grill, and Crocker-Citizens Bank. Desmond's, a veteran of the Valley and Santa Ana complexes, opened as well.

COME TO A NEW WORLD

OF FASHION...IN

BULLOCK'S FASHION SQUARE
D E L   A M O
TORRANCE

HAWTHORNE BLVD. AT CARSON   TORRANCE, CALIFORNIA

A unique feature of the square was La Casita ("little house" in Spanish). La Casita was considered the heart of Del Amo Fashion Square. The little Spanish-style building was slightly raised off the ground and decorated with hanging iron lanterns. It was later dedicated to the community for use by civic, cultural, and community groups. The site was also perfect for visits with Santa at Christmas. The fashion court outside of La Casita hosted fashion shows, flower and art displays, and concerts.

La Habra Fashion Square was the last of the four stores Bullock's would build. Opening as a completely developed project, La Habra would be the first to have another major anchor open with the Bullock's branch. A 271,000-square-foot, three-level building, along with a 120,000-square-foot branch of Buffum's, opened in August 1968. A collection of 30 shops, a La Casita community room, theaters, and a Joseph Magnin outlet rounded out the project. Welton Becket and Associates were the project's architects.

La Habra Fashion Square was considered the most beautiful of them all, with its lush landscaping and its architecture featuring Spanish red-tile roofs. Its uniform layout in a now-traditional shopping center design produced a dramatic setting leading to each department store.

Bullock's main floor was very elegant, with huge hand-painted murals, mirrored glass, and overhead chandeliers. Although La Habra was beautiful in its design and offerings, the center had issues from its opening. La Habra Fashion Square was built at the intersection of Highway 39, Beach Boulevard, and Imperial Highway. In the late 1960s, Orange County was dealing with traffic problems that Los Angeles had been having for some time. A major north-south freeway was needed to help with the increasing population. Highway 39 from Huntington Beach to La Habra to the north would make a perfect thoroughfare.

In 1984, the City of Santa Ana began the process of redeveloping Fashion Square into a new retail, office, and residential space. Main Place Santa Ana, a two-level, enclosed regional mall, opened in September 1987. Bullock's, Nordstrom, and Robinson's were the major commercial anchors. Only the Bullock's building and a shell of the I. Magnin store remained in the newly designed mall. (Courtesy of Santa Ana History Room, Santa Ana Public Library.)

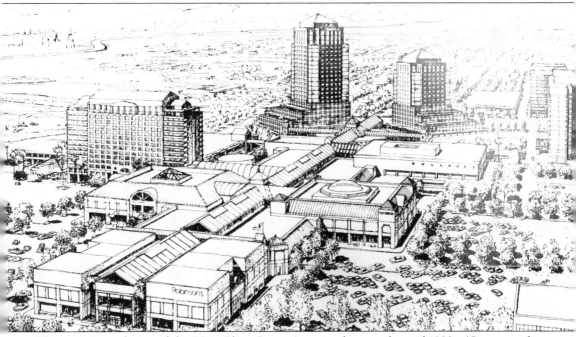

This artistic rendering of the Main Place Santa Ana site dates to the mid-1980s. (Courtesy of Santa Ana History Room, Santa Ana Public Library.)

William Pereira and Charles Luckman were Los Angeles–based architects whose work on the Disneyland Hotel and Theme Building at Los Angeles International Airport were well known. The team designed many homes, as well as numerous department stores, including Robinson's Beverly Hills. Pereira himself was responsible for many of the California Mission–inspired Robinson's stores, while Luckman designed for The Broadway and Weinstock's. Shown here is Bullock's Santa Ana.

Pereira and Luckman worked closely with Bullock's interior designers and artists. Every aspect of the store would be detailed through the use of architectural models, drawings, and blueprints. Shown here is a design for Santa Ana's third-floor galleria, as viewed from the main elevator shaft.

Five

BULLOCK'S

ITS MANY STORES

P.G. Winnett was the guiding force behind the Bullock's organization. After John Bullock's passing in 1933, Winnett became president of the company and spearheaded its expansion in all aspects of retailing. His notes and store objectives are endless and precise. He was responsible for Bullocks Wilshire, the shops in Westwood, Palm Springs, and Pasadena, and countless work at the downtown store, in addition to the merger with I. Magnin. He personally visited each store weekly, speaking with store personnel and passing out chocolate kisses.

In January 1944, I. Magnin & Co, the San Francisco–based luxury retailer, was seeking a suitable buyer to supplement its continued operation. With John and Grover Magnin approaching their golden years, a strong buyer was needed. P.G. Winnett had long admired the I. Magnin & Co. stores, and he stepped forward as a buyer.

Federated Department Stores of Cincinnati was a giant operator of stores in the Midwest, the South, and the East Coast. Filene's, Sanger's, Burdines, The Bon Marché, and Bloomingdale's operated under Federated's banner. They did not, however, have a presence in California. The company thus had its eye on the highly profitable Bullock's-Magnin operation.

In 1964, longtime principal stockholder and Bullock's board director P.G. Winnett was entangled in a very public proxy fight. The company's board of directors believed a merger with Fred Lazarus's Federated group would be in their best interest. Winnett felt otherwise, as Bullock's had a better earnings record than did Federated's units, and it also had a higher book value. Winnett feared that Bullock's would lose its local buying power and its touch with its California patrons. Winnett's son-in-law and a board member, Walter Candy, gained the most support for the merger. Candy felt that stockholders would receive big dividends, even at a proposed 1.4 to 1 ratio.

Winnett's struggle to keep Bullock's-Magnin its own operation was a losing battle. Many in the company believed the merger was needed to remain competitive with other retailers. After four months of bitter debate, Winnett was ousted, and Candy was elected chairman of Federated's new Bullock's-Magnin division.

P.G. Winnett, cofounder of the grand Bullock's stores, spent much of his "retirement" visiting his branch stores each day, holding a lifelong contract as an advisor to Bullock's Inc. Winnett was known to walk the stores' sales floors and salons while chatting with staff, store managers, and patrons. He would often take lunch in one of the stores' tearooms. Winnett passed away at his home on July 18, 1968, at the age of 83.

The Desert Inn location proved very popular with several expansions, until a new store was built in 1947 at 141 South Palm Canyon Drive. Designed by architects Walter Wurderman and William Becket, the striking structure was built in the late Modern style. In the late 1960s, this smaller location was converted to a Bullocks Wilshire specialty store.

The Palm Springs location had floor-to-ceiling display windows that ushered in the bright desert sun. Overhangs protected displays and enclosed merchandise. As with Pasadena, all of the store's furniture and displays were custom-built for the store and were modular and movable.

Downtown Palm Springs, Palm Canyon Drive, La Plaza, and Bullock's made for a resort shopping district of its own. Many Los Angeles–area stores operated "resort" shops that were only opened seasonally, from October to May. Desmond's, Robinson's, Joseph Magnin, and others lined sunny Palm Canyon for years.

This May 14, 1932, advertisement announces the opening of the first Westwood Bullock's. This shop was part of the larger Westwood Village development owned by the Janss Corporation. Westwood Village was designed as a shopping, service, and entertainment center to serve the growing UCLA campus and west Los Angeles. Janss Corp controlled every aspect of the village development, including building size and height.

Originally, Bullock's Westwood Village had a lush garden patio located just off the tearoom. Tearooms and the use of landscaped areas would be a Bullock's tradition in most of its stores for years to come.

On January 22, 1939, the company announced the fourth enlargement of the original Bullock's store in Westwood Village by P.G. Winnett. Total investment was $1 million, with original architects John and Donald Parkinson preparing the plans for the building's expansion. Architect A.R. Brandner designed the new interiors, featuring a top-floor tearoom and a panoramic patio.

The new Westwood store, built in a contemporary design, occupied a sloping, four-acre site between Weyburn and Le Conte Avenues. The store took advantage of the differential in grade to provide two principal merchandising levels. The front is formed by a wide colonnade supporting a dramatic, curved entablature.

For years, Westwood Village had problems with automobile parking, as most establishments had no parking facilities of their own. To remedy the situation for the new Bullock's store, architects designed tiered parking on the roof, which could be reached via ramps from the street. Both parking areas were connected to the store and tearoom.

The Lotus Tea Room menu at Bullock's Westwood included specialties such as lotus Polynesian salad, Villager luncheon, baked cheese soufflé, and breast of chicken à la Maryland. The desserts included lemon cake, baked custard, and brandy rum fruitcake.

The large, 350-seat Lotus Tea Room had its own entry and parking on the roof of the store. Expansive, wraparound windows brought in natural light and afforded patrons spectacular views of the UCLA campus and the Santa Monica Mountains. Botanical-inspired murals by Annett Honeywell flanked both sides of the room, which also had a decorative pond and a skylight in the center.

This is the Westwood reception area tea room. This modern store was designed with many interior features, including indoor planters, custom-designed furniture and display cases, and an abundant amount of art. Etched-glass screens and two heavy bronze sculptures by artist Bernard Rosenthal were found throughout the store.

Westwood's tile detail included Hermosa Faience tile, 12 inches by 12 inches, handmade by Gladding McBean. Thousands of these tiles were made, and they clad three sides of the building, including the rooftop tearoom. Gladding McBean was a prolific manufacturer of ceramics for building architecture. The firm provided decorative elements for countless structures across the country.

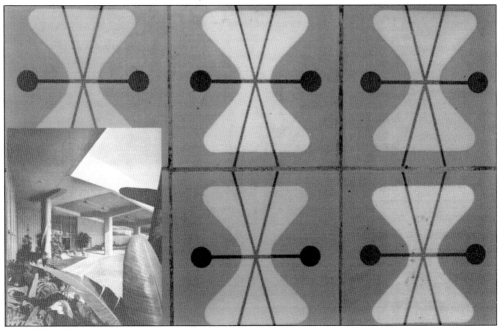

This pre-opening photograph depicts ground-level parking, the entrance, and the loading dock of Bullock's Lakewood. Both the Lakewood and Torrance stores were built to identical designs and under similar conditions. The ground, naturally sloping, allowed for multiple store entrances on different levels of the four-story building.

This pre-opening photograph of Bullock's Lakewood depicts its west-facing parking area and second-level entrances.

Lakewood Center had opened in 1951 as the first part of the largest planned community center in the nation. May Co., Butler Brothers, and many other retailers, restaurants, and city services rounded out the complex's tenants. From its early stages, Lakewood Center would be parceled into areas dedicated to retail, medical, civic, and social functions. Bullock's placement away from the main mall was the result of another retailer's strict agreement with the center.

a new fashion spot...

a new bullock's

BULLOCK'S LAKEWOOD
OPENS TODAY
MONDAY APRIL 26TH

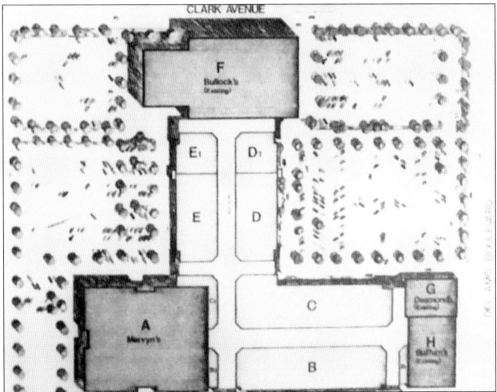

In 1979, Lakewood Center announced plans to expand the mall to include a separate second mall, an 89,000-square-foot Mervyn's store with 70 new shops linking the existing Buffums' and Bullock's stores. The second mall was never built; only the Mervyn's wing was constructed.

On Monday, January 17, 1994, a magnitude 6.8 earthquake shook Southern California at 4:31 a.m. The Northridge Bullock's store (pictured here) collapsed under the force of the quake and was rebuilt but in a different style. Fortunately, no one was injured in the destroyed store. Thousands of buildings and much municipal infrastructure were damaged, with costs exceeding $10 billion.

The $60 million Northridge Fashion Center, a complex of "commerce and community," opened in September 1971. The Broadway and Sears stores would open by November of that year.

Bullock's Costa Mesa South Coast Plaza opened in 1967 as an indoor center, with May Co. and Sears as its anchors. By 1973, the center's high sales brought the addition of Bullock's and a wing of higher-end shops. I. Magnin, Saks, and California's first Nordstrom had all opened by 1979, giving the plaza a special niche in luxury retailing. (Courtesy Costa Mesa Historical Society.)

Shown here is the interior of the Costa Mesa store, which is identical in layout to the Mission Valley store. Open space for escalators made use of the three-story building, which was finished in natural materials and designed with earthy tones; heavy-texture brick and rough wood were used. The ceiling was done in black, with clear glass filament set in crystal globes. During this time, Bullock's stores embraced the consumers' preference for a darker shopping environment, with emphasis on product spotlighting.

Bullock's South Coast became the top-grossing location within the 22-store chain.

The Woodland Hills Promenade was chosen as the first newly built Bullocks Wilshire branch. Opened on August 20, 1973, the store combined the classic chic of the 1929 original with trendy 1970s glitz. This was most apparent in its architecture, interior design, and the display and selling of high-fashion merchandise. The new store not only drew inspiration from the Wilshire classic, but it actually used hardware and vintage design elements from the 1929 store itself. According to Walter Bergquist, "The concept we wanted was a store that would provide modern surroundings for fashionable quality merchandise Bullocks Wilshire has offered Southern Californians for nearly half a century." Welton Becket and Associates were the architects responsible for this inspiring building. The exterior of the two-level, 80,000-square-foot store was constructed via an unconventional use of white masonry. The unusual sloping brick walls gave the store an informal, sunny, white-washed appearance.

In the exact center of the Woodland Hills Promenade, serving as the building's visual reference point, was a two-story garden court with elegant stairwell, potted palms, and dual exposed glass elevators.

In adhering to the store's rich Art Deco styling, the interior was detailed in wall coverings, etched glass, glass panes, display cases, and antique objects. The art nouveau tearoom, with its mocha style, etched glass walls, chandeliers, and hand-painted decorations, whisked patrons back to a turn-of-the-century Parisian café.

The Woodland Hills Promenade emphasized lifestyle, with its many sales departments clustered around each other and the center of the store. The departments reflected the activities of the store's patrons, male or female, and appealed to all ages.

The art nouveau tearoom continued the Bullock's tradition, as this charming, 18th-century-style Parisian cafe was decorated with etched mirrored panels, hand-painted appointments, and chandeliers of flower-shaped glass.

For the second Bullocks Wilshire branch, the wealthy seaside community of Newport Beach in Orange County was selected. Newport Center, Fashion Island was a well-established shopping and financial center, having opened in September 1967. After 10 years, Fashion Island saw its first major expansion, including the Bullocks Wilshire store and a complementary wing of 25 specialty shops.

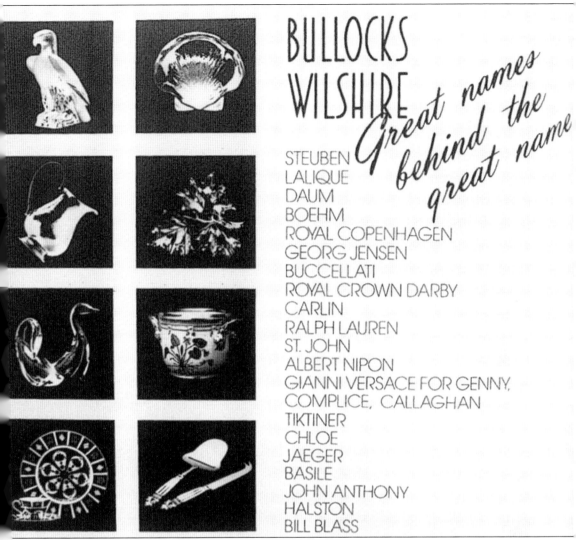

BULLOCKS
WILSHIRE

Great names behind the great name

STEUBEN
LALIQUE
DAUM
BOEHM
ROYAL COPENHAGEN
GEORG JENSEN
BUCCELLATI
ROYAL CROWN DARBY
CARLIN
RALPH LAUREN
ST. JOHN
ALBERT NIPON
GIANNI VERSACE FOR GENNY,
COMPLICE, CALLAGHAN
TIKTINER
CHLOE
JAEGER
BASILE
JOHN ANTHONY
HALSTON
BILL BLASS

The expansion by Bullock's into Newport Beach was fueled in part by rival South Coast Plaza's growing reputation. Commenting on the Fashion Island store, Federated Department Store's vice chairman, Howard Goldfeder, vowed, "The new store will offer residents of the Newport Beach area the highest quality merchandise and the latest in high fashion in a dramatic setting of contemporary elegance."

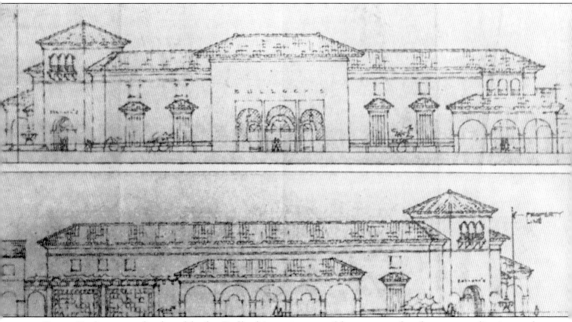

Santa Barbara city leaders felt the Bullock's project would augment the downtown district and revitalize the area. Many business owners and residents felt otherwise. For the project to go forward, local businesses would be forced to relocate or close altogether. Others argued that the downtown area was not in a state of decline and that retail sales were among the highest in the state. Also, the Bullock's store might siphon away sales from local merchants. To finance the project, the city placed bonds up to $23 million on the November ballot. The move saw fierce opposition. Voters rejected the proposal, and in early 1984, Federated Department Stores withdrew its funding for the downtown store.

Bullock's Palo Alto, located in the Stanford Shopping Center in Palo Alto, was the company's first Northern California store. The Bullock's ideal and merchandising concept had worked so well in Southern California for over 60 years that its parent, Federated Department Stores, felt it could work just as well in the Bay Area. After years of planning and marketing research, Federated, which owned the Bullock's/I. Magnin chains, believed the upper-class community of Palo Alto would support a higher-end Bullock's outlet. I. Magnin had opened a branch at the center in 1956, and its profitability eventually led to the location doubling its size.

The 150,000-square-foot Palo Alto store was announced in June 1970, with site preparation slated for February 1971. Bullock's North, a separate division from Bullock's in Southern California, set up business and clerical operations on California Avenue. In late summer 1971, the headquarters was moved to a combination office and receiving warehouse building on Constitution Drive in Bohannon Industrial Park.

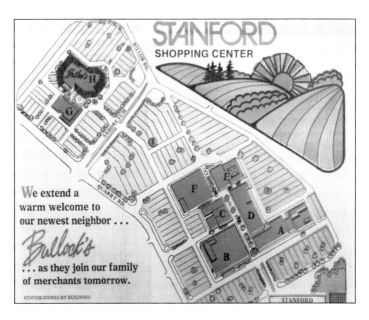

The final Bullock's store, at Burbank Media City Center Mall, opened on September 2, 1992. The building was designed by the New York firm of Brennan Beer Gorman/Architects. Much care was given to the building's Art Deco–inspired facade. Twin towers rising 65 feet in the air flanked three stylized windows with brass entry doors. The imposing structure harkened back to the 1929 Bullocks Wilshire store. The interior of the store was no less spectacular, with highly polished marble, custom display cases, and a central escalator well with a dramatic skylight finished in pear wood paneling. Bullock's became Macy's on Monday April 29, 1996, and Federated Department Stores began the task of changing the 23 Bullock's stores to the Macy's nameplate. By May of that year, Bullock's had become part of California's retail past. (Courtesy of Berliner Studio.)

Magnin-Bullock's Merger Unites Coast Quality Stores

Bullock's and Magnin's. Coast Stores. Merging

continued from Page One

Coast. With the merging of the Magnin stores, Bullock's expansion from a southern California operation into a coastwide organization, now operating stores in Los Angeles, Beverly Hills, San Francisco, Oakland, Pasadena, Santa Barbara, Coronado, Westwood and Palm Springs, point to the further expansion of the organization.

"We look forward proudly to the future of these two old and distinguished names in retailing," stated Mr. A. Magnin. "One of the most definite results of the affiliation is the leadership and prestige which the Magnin organization will enjoy intimately in the quality markets of the United States, and after the war the leading markets in all parts of the world."

Both Bullock's, Inc., and I. Magnin hold a prominent position among the world's fine retail organizations. Magnin's has persistently followed a policy of highly specialized merchandise for a discriminating middle and upper bracket clientele. The rapidly expanding volume and inclusion of new classifications of merchandise to its scope have not weakened its strict adherence to its ideal of quality and service.

Magnin's is known from coast to coast as a foremost creator and authority on fashions for women. It has confined its operations to the retailing of distinctive ready-to-wear, accessories, children's apparel and art wares.

Prior to the affiliation of the Magnin stores, Bullock's had concentrated its efforts in the Los Angeles area. Bullock's Downtown, located at the heart of the metropolitan district, is one of the largest complete retail stores in the nation. Bullock's Wilshire, in the fashionable Wilshire center, a shopping district, serves a selected clientele with men's, women's and children's apparel, accessories, gift and art objects. Bullock's Westwood is adjacent to the campus of the University of California at Los Angeles community. Bullock's Palm Springs, on the grounds of the Desert Inn, is a complete resort shop for vacationists.

Magnin & Co. stores have extended from an original location in

P. G. Winnett
President of Bullock's, Los Angeles, the merger of which with I. Magnin & Co., is pending.

New York Executives

Magnin's and Bullock's both maintain their own offices in New York.

Bullock's office is headed by Blanche Baumgarten, and is a separate office within the AMC, occupying space on the ninth floor of the building at 1440 Broadway, which is in the same building in which the AMC offices are housed.

Magnin's offices are on 37th street in the office building which adjoins the Franklin Simon store on Fifth avenue. John Magnin, who spends much of his time in New York, is most active in the company's affairs here. Samuel Siegel is the office manager for Magnin's.

The possibilities that both offices might be maintained were indicated by the statement issued by heads of the two store organizations on the Coast that the separate buying staffs would be maintained.

E. John Magnin
President of I. Magnin & Co., whose chain of fine specialty shops on the Coast is now pending merging with Bullock's.

Founded in 1907, Bullock's Survived Panic Year

It was a dreary, rainy day on March 4, 1907, when the retail institution which became Bullock's, Inc., opened its doors at the corner of Broadway and 7th streets, Los Angeles, then on the outskirts of the business district. The founder of the business and its guiding light was John G. Bullock, who left the Broadway Dept. Store where he had been superintendent, to start his own business. He took with him P. G. Winnett.

In July, seemingly from out of nowhere, came the financial panic of 1907, which swept away two other Los Angeles dry goods stores but left Bullock's solvent.

Having weathered that storm, the saga of Bullock's became one of expansion on expansion, from 1912 down through the years. That year saw a 10-story building erected.

The firm was incorporated in 1927, and in the years immediately following built branch stores and invested from San Francisco to include important cities up and down the Pacific Coast. The company's largest stores are operated in San Francisco and Los Angeles, with other stores in Seattle, Oakland, Santa Barbara, Beverly Hills, Pasadena and Coronado.

in subsidiary companies some of which it later dissolved.

Officers of Bullock's, Inc., are P. G. Winnett, president; W. A. Holt, vice-president; W. E. Goodhue, vice-president and treasurer; M. E. Arnett, secretary. Directors include Mr. Winnett, Mr. Holt, Mr. Goodhue, S. F. Macfarlane, and J. D. Brady.

For the year ended Jan. 31, 1943, Bullock's reported net sales of $35,303,215.

Prophetic Quality In "Bullock's Ideals"

There's a prophetic quality in view of today's news to the first of Bullock's Ideals as stated some years back: "To build a business that will never know completion but that will advance continually to meet advancing conditions.

"To develop stocks and services to a maximum degree.

"To create a personality that will be known for its strength and friendliness.

"To arrange and coordinate activities to the end of winning confidence by meriting it.

"To strive always to secure the satisfaction of every customer."

Magnin's 65-Year Growth A Retail Trade Romance

I. Magnin & Co., with its present chain of stores covering the coast from Seattle to Coronado, is reputed one of the largest distributors of women's and misses' fine apparel in the country. The growth of the present company from a single small notion store in an obscure district in San Francisco more than 65 years ago constitutes one of the romances of the retail world.

Through more than 65 years of existence, I. Magnin & Co. has adhered tenaciously to a policy of buying and selling quality apparel. This Pacific Coast retail institution has voluntarily chosen to follow an individualistic merchandising program which has assumed that a certain segment of the population will never tamper with tried-and-true standards, no matter what the exigencies of the moment.

An invariable rule of the organization, according to E. John Magnin, president, has been to "mind its own business." Neither he nor his business, he has stated, are the least bit interested in what other stores are doing. "Actuating this resolve is a desire to keep the needs of the particular clientele clearly in mind and not be swayed in an adverse preference, Mr. Magnin has as... Other officers of the Magnin are Grover A. Magnin, first vice-president; Mary Ann Magnin, Carpenter, Edwin Joseph, vice-president; Samuel Magnin, secretary-treasurer. Directors include abovementioned members of the Magnin family, Mr. Carpenter, Lilienthal, Jr., Dean Witter, Joseph.

For the year ended Dec...Magnin... reported net sales of $479,742.

Magnin stores are located in San Francisco, Oakland, Seattle, Los Angeles, Pasadena, Beverly Hills, Santa Barbara and Coronado.

Trade's Interest Great

In January 1944, I. Magnin, the San Francisco–based luxury retailer, was seeking a suitable buyer to keep its operation going. P.G. Winnett had long admired the Magnin stores. Feeling that they would be a good fit, he stepped in as a buyer. (Courtesy of *Women's Wear Daily*.)

This is the I. Magnin flagship store on Union Square in San Francisco. Magnin began in 1876 as a small needlepoint and notions shop, and grew to become one of the most fashionable shops on the West Coast. I. Magnin was started by Mary Ann Magnin, but it was named for her husband, Isaac. Her sons John and Grover oversaw the rise of this grand store.

BULLOCK'S
DEPARTMENT STORES
INCOMPLETE LISTING

Downtown: March 4, 1907
Palm Springs, Desert Inn: November 20, 1930
Pasadena: September 10, 1947
Westwood: September 5, 1951
Santa Ana: September 17, 1958
San Fernando Valley/Sherman Oaks: April 30, 1962
Lakewood: April 26, 1965
Del Amo: September 12, 1966
La Habra: August 12, 1968
Northridge: September 10, 1971
South Coast Plaza: September 26, 1973
San Diego/Mission Valley: February 19, 1975
West Covina: September 25, 1975
Century City: September 9, 1976
Scottsdale (AZ): January 31, 1977

Bullocks Wilshire Locations:
  Wilshire: September 24, 1929
  Palm Springs: October 18, 1947
  Woodland Hills: August 20, 1973
  Newport Beach: August 1, 1977
  La Jolla: August 20, 1979
  Palos Verdes: September 28, 1981
  Palm Desert: February 7, 1987

Chris-Town (AZ): November 1987
Mission Viejo: March 3, 1980
Carlsbad: October 2, 1980
Las Vegas: February 14, 1981
Beverly Center: February 4, 1982
Manhattan Beach: February 4, 1982
Thousand Oaks: August 4, 1983
Grossmont: September 15, 1983
Palm Desert: November 3, 1983
7th Market Place: August 4, 1986
South Coast Plaza Men's Store: July 16, 1991
Burbank: September 2, 1992
Beverly Center Men's Store: November 10, 1993
Woodland Hills: November 10, 1993

DISCOVER THOUSANDS OF LOCAL HISTORY BOOKS FEATURING MILLIONS OF VINTAGE IMAGES

Arcadia Publishing, the leading local history publisher in the United States, is committed to making history accessible and meaningful through publishing books that celebrate and preserve the heritage of America's people and places.

Find more books like this at
www.arcadiapublishing.com

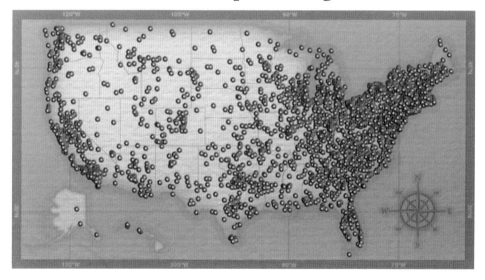

Search for your hometown history, your old stomping grounds, and even your favorite sports team.

Consistent with our mission to preserve history on a local level, this book was printed in South Carolina on American-made paper and manufactured entirely in the United States. Products carrying the accredited Forest Stewardship Council (FSC) label are printed on 100 percent FSC-certified paper.

MADE IN THE USA